COUNTRY WALKS

"Walking yields a greater closeness to the earth, an
independence. The solid thud of boots on the path means
freedom to stop and admire a flower, to move at one's
own speed, to rejoice in crossing a stream on risky
stepping stones, to explore off the trail, to get
a close-up of dew jewelling the grass."

JOHN MUIR

Stoddart

The Niagara Escarpment

COUNTRY WALKS

Ross McLean   Anne Craik   John Sherk

A Boston Mills Press Book

Canadian Cataloguing in Publication Data

McLean, Ross E.

COUNTRY WALKS:
The Niagara Escarpment

Includes bibliographical references and index.
  ISBN 1-55046-102-8

1. Hiking – Niagara Escarpment – Guidebooks.
2. Trails – Niagara Escarpment – Guidebooks.
3. Niagara Escarpment – Guidebooks.
I. Craik, Anne II. Sherk, John.
III. Title.

FC3095.N5A3 1994   917.1304'4
C94-930283-X
F1059.N48M35 1994

Design and Typography by Daniel Crack,
Kinetics Design & Illustration
Printed in Canada

First published in 1994 by
Stoddart Publishing Co. Limited
34 Lesmill Road
Toronto, Canada   M3B 2T6
(416) 445-3333

A BOSTON MILLS PRESS BOOK
The Boston Mills Press
132 Main Street
Erin, Ontario   N0B 1T0

The publisher gratefully acknowledges the support of
the Canada Council, Ontario Ministry of Culture and
Communications, Ontario Arts Council and Ontario
Publishing Centre in the development of writing and
publishing in Canada.

Second printing March 1995

Front cover:
The woods at Niagara Glen in the spring
– Richard Armstrong

Back cover:
Members of the Bruce Trail Association
on a beginners' hike.
– Richard Armstrong

Page 1:
– Lorne Geddes

Pages 2-3:
Looking across Beaver Valley to Old Baldy.
– Lorne Geddes

Contents

Dedicated to Raymond Lowes, the Federation of Ontario Naturalists and the pioneer builders of the Bruce Trail, for their foresight in recognizing the importance of the Niagara Escarpment and the need to protect it.

Acknowledgments

Thanks are due to a number of people whose willing assistance has enabled us to produce this book. We are especially indebted to David Turrell, Kay Kelly, Richard Armstrong, Lorne Geddes, Richard Murzin, Sheila Gatis, Bev Matheson, Jean Turnbull and Ruth Forsythe. To family members and friends who as hiking companions, have provided unfailing encouragement and advice, we owe an enormous debt of gratitude.

The authors express their appreciation to staff members of the following organizations who willingly provided us with photographs, pamphlets and brochures, and also lent their time and expertise to help us gather illustrations and information for *Country Walks:*

Archives of Ontario, Bruce County Historical Society, Bruce Trail Association, Canadian Parks Service, Credit Valley Conservation Authority, County of Bruce Museum, County of Grey – Owen Sound Museum, Collingwood Museum, Dufferin County Museum, Georgian Triangle Tourist Association and Convention Bureau, Federation of Ontario Naturalists, Grey-Bruce Tourist Association, Grey-Sauble Conservation Authority, Halton Region Conservation Authority, Hamilton Naturalists' Club, Hamilton Region Conservation Authority, Ministry of Agriculture and Food, Ministry of Natural Resources, Niagara Escarpment Commission, Niagara Falls Heritage Foundation, Niagara Parks Commission, Niagara Peninsula Conservation Authority, Owen Sound Visitor and Convention Bureau, Region of Peel Archives, Region of Peel Art Gallery, Royal Botanical Gardens, Tobermory Chamber of Commerce, and Township of Collingwood Archives.

Preface

We have written *Country Walks: The Niagara Escarpment* in response to the many queries that have been addressed to us as active hikers and trail volunteers. Time and again we have been asked: How do I find the Bruce Trail? If I go out for a day hike, will I have to retrace my steps? Are all the trails difficult? Do I need to buy expensive hiking boots? Are there any trails suitable for small children? Are there places to camp or to stay near the trails?

Such questions made us feel that public knowledge about hiking along the Niagara Escarpment and on the Bruce Trail is meagre, to say the least, and we believe that people will be glad to know that they can find a great variety and abundance of beautiful hikes along the entire length of the Niagara Escarpment.

We have tried to create a book that is easy to use and that provides answers to practical, essential questions. Most of the hikes we have selected are loops, hikes that take you back to your starting point without backtracking over the same ground. The range of hikes varies widely; some short, some long, some easy, some moderate, one or two strenuous. We believe that our selection will appeal to a wide range of people: families, those who have never hiked but would like to start, those who want to mix hiking with other recreational activities, and more experienced hikers who are looking for new challenges. We hope that the hike descriptions, photographs and maps will give you clear and accurate information about what you can expect to find. We also hope that they will tempt you to venture out to find it.

We are acutely aware that we have not covered everything. For example, in each hike description we have been able to make no more than passing reference to flora and fauna. On your walks, you will encounter a tremendous diversity of plants and animals; some of them rare, some of them unique to the escarpment habitat. Some thirty-seven species of ferns and forty species of orchids flourish along the length of the escarpment. Plants and animals usually found much further south thrive in the Carolinian forest zone of the Niagara-Hamilton region, and more than three hundred species of birds make the escarpment a bird-watcher's paradise. You can find enormous pleasure in learning where to look for certain species and how to recognize them. If you take good field guides and a pair of binoculars with you on your walks, you will gradually discover the riches of the natural world that await you along the escarpment.

Enjoy its treasures, but please, always abide by the Trail Users' Code and strive to ensure that the habitat remains intact for future generations.

Happy hiking!

Introduction

THE NIAGARA ESCARPMENT

In 1990, the Niagara Escarpment was formally recognized by the United Nations as an ecologically important area. It was declared a World Biosphere Reserve, a designation that identified its unique natural features as being worthy of protection and preservation for all time and for all people. With this designation by UNESCO, it joined such exotic locales as the Galapagos Islands and the Serengeti National Park.

The Niagara Escarpment is an unbroken ridge across the Southern Ontario landscape, running 725 kilometres from historic Queenston Heights on the Niagara River to Flowerpot Island in Fathom Five National Marine Park off the northern tip of the Bruce Peninsula.

A priceless geological gem formed over 400 million years ago, the escarpment is also a vast repository of our natural and cultural heritage. From the shipwrecks beneath the clear waters of Georgian Bay to the battle sites of the Niagara Peninsula where nation once confronted nation, the escarpment reveals much of Ontario's history. It also offers a rich diversity of natural beauty—magnificent waterfalls, fascinating landforms, rare plants and elusive wildlife.

The Niagara Escarpment is many things to many people; everyone views it from their own perspective. But foremost, it is a winding ribbon of natural beauty, and one of Ontario's prime recreational areas. Each of us bears part of the responsibility of ensuring that it is preserved in perpetuity.

You are invited to experience its richness and to explore its diversity.

THE GEOLOGY OF THE NIAGARA ESCARPMENT

In our descriptions throughout the book, we often refer to the geology of the Niagara Escarpment. We do this because we have found that hikers, by and large, are curious people. When they peer into a gorge or descend into the depth of a large inland cave, they are not content simply to look and admire, but immediately ask how and why and when? Along the Niagara Escarpment, there are a myriad of fascinating geological formations; how they come to be there is an equally fascinating story and one that we feel the curious explorer will want to know. We hope that this brief introduction to the geology of the escarpment will provide a useful background to our more specific chapter-by-chapter comments on particular landforms.

The Niagara Escarpment is the result of two opposing geological processes, deposition and erosion. Its story begins about 450 million years ago when an upheaval in the earth's crust resulted in the rise of a great range of mountains along the eastern edge of North America. Over time, as these mountains succumbed to the force of rain, wind and ice, fast-flowing rivers carried the eroded material westward.

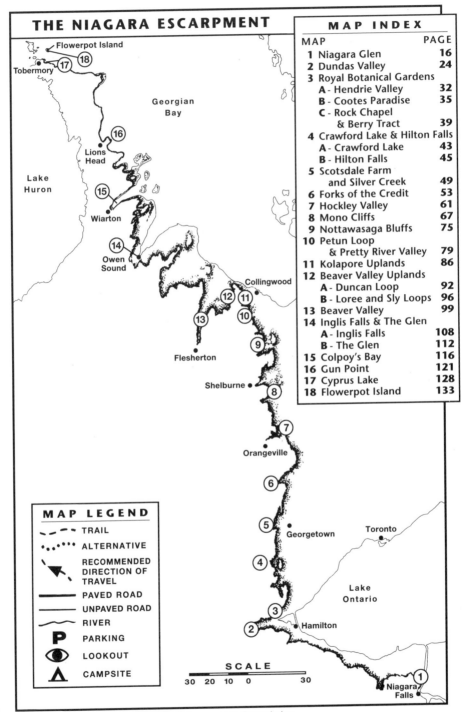

THE NIAGARA ESCARPMENT

Flowerpot Island
Tobermory
Georgian Bay
Lake Huron
Lions Head
Wiarton
Owen Sound
Collingwood
Flesherton
Shelburne
Orangeville
Georgetown
Toronto
Lake Ontario
Hamilton
Niagara Falls

MAP LEGEND

- – – – TRAIL
- •••••• ALTERNATIVE
- ◢ RECOMMENDED DIRECTION OF TRAVEL
- ▬▬ PAVED ROAD
- ─── UNPAVED ROAD
- ～～ RIVER
- **P** PARKING
- ◉ LOOKOUT
- ▲ CAMPSITE

SCALE

30 20 10 0   30

– Map outline courtesy of the Niagara Escarpment Commission

They flowed towards a large shallow sea that lay in a saucer-shaped depression centred in the state of Michigan and known as the Michigan Basin. When they met this sea, the rivers deposited their sediment, forming an immense river delta. This deltaic sediment gradually hardened into the red shale and sandstone rocks that today form the base of the escarpment.

Then, approximately 425 million years ago, the sea rose, flooding the delta and forming a warm, clear ocean. Coral reefs developed and plant and animal life flourished. As these organisms died, their calcium-rich remains fell to the ocean floor and were compressed into layer upon layer of limestone.

After ten million years or so, further changes in the earth's crust caused the Michigan Basin to rise. The vast sea began to shrink, becoming shallower and shallower, with increasing concentrations of salt and magnesium. As magnesium-rich water seeped into the porous limestone, a chemical bonding process occurred. Limestone and magnesium combined to form dolostone, a hard, erosion-resistant rock that today forms the cap-rock of the escarpment.

Over the next 100 million years, the seas withdrew completely, leaving an immense flat plain, which in its turn was reshaped by the forces of erosion. Rivers cut through the body of the plain, carving out narrow valleys, and along its outer edge, wind, ice and surface water slowly removed the weaker shale layers underlying the more resistant cap-rock. Large blocks of dolostone broke off the top, creating the vertical face that characterizes the escarpment today.

Next came the ice ages. Four times within the past two million years, the escarpment has been buried under 2 to 3 kilometres of ice, which melted away only twelve thousand years ago. Moving ice scraped rock layers from the top of the escarpment, broadened valley floors and steepened their sides, leaving U-shaped formations. When the glaciers retreated, they deposited materials that they had scraped and pushed from areas to the north. These deposits, now covering the underlying rock in layers up to a 100 metres thick, are called glacial till. In places such as the highlands of Central Ontario, the till makes it difficult to recognize the edge of the scarp.

Since the departure of the glaciers, the forces of erosion have continued to change the face of the escarpment. Along the shores of Georgian Bay in the Bruce Peninsula, for example, caves, headlands and sea stacks have been formed by buffeting waves. To the south, the force of running water has carved the Niagara Gorge during the past thirteen thousand years. The chemical action of water slowly dissolving the porous dolostone has created karst features such as caves and crevices. And as a reminder that erosion never ceases, when you walk along the exposed face of the escarpment, patches of gleaming white will tell you that frost action has recently broken off another piece of rock, hurling it to the talus slope below.

Thus the face of the Niagara Escarpment continues to change as it yields to the inexorable forces of geology.

THE BRUCE TRAIL

The chain that holds together most of the hiking paths described in *Country Walks: The Niagara Escarpment* is the Bruce Trail.

Extending the length of the escarpment, the Bruce Trail is a 780-kilometre footpath which was built and today is maintained by volunteers. It was the result of the vision of one man, Ray Lowes, who dreamt of a natural corridor running the length of Southern Ontario's most significant landform.

Today, from its southern terminus at Queenston Heights, the Bruce Trail crosses the fruitlands of the Niagara Peninsula, the beautiful Dundas Valley and the city of Hamilton, the rolling Caledon Hills, the highlands of Central Ontario, the Blue Mountains of Collingwood, and the pastoral charm of the Beaver Valley. It continues northward to Owen Sound, Wiarton and Lion's Head and finally to the spectacular cliffs of the Bruce Peninsula National Park along the Georgian Bay shoreline. At the fishing village of Tobermory, a cairn overlooking the harbour marks the trail's northern terminus.

Although close to major population centres, the trail can transport you into a world where the pace is slower, where there is time to stop and notice nature's smaller wonders—a place of solitude and charm. The trail passes waterfalls and scenic viewpoints; it wanders alongside rivers, farms and lighthouses; it takes you over headlands and through gorges; and best of all, it lets you take your time.

From the time that Ray Lowes first put forward his idea for a trail in 1959, the Bruce Trail has received support from thousands of enthusiastic volunteers. The trail was built by volunteers, and every year they head out in their hundreds to clear the treadway, build and repair bridges and boardwalks, and repaint blazes. They all belong to the Bruce Trail Association (the BTA), an organization committed to preserving the Niagara Escarpment and securing a permanent trail that everyone can use. Without the BTA, most of the walks described in this book would not exist. When you have explored a few of them, you may feel you want to become a member and make your own contribution to keeping them intact forever.

For more information on the Bruce Trail, contact:
The Bruce Trail Association
Box 857
Hamilton, Ontario L8N 3N9
Telephone 1-800-665-HIKE

FOLLOWING THE TRAILS

The trails are not difficult to follow. The Bruce Trail is marked along its route with white blazes, 15 centimetres high by 5 centimetres wide, painted on trees and fence posts. Usually, as you hike the trail, the blazes face you, and if the path ahead is not obvious, another blaze is visible from the first. On a straightforward path where there is no confusion, however, the blazes may be infrequent.

A double blaze (one above the other) indicates a turn. Sometimes, the upper blaze is offset in the new direction of travel; otherwise, look for the next single blaze to either the left or right.

Bruce Trail side trails are blazed in blue and may lead to lookouts, drinking water or campsites, or form circular hikes. You may occasionally encounter yellow blazes leading off a blue-blazed side trail. Diamond-shaped Bruce Trail symbols and access signs also mark the trail.

Sometimes a section of the trail is rerouted as either an improvement or a necessity because of a landowner's request. If you come across a newly rerouted section, *follow the blazes,* not where you thought the trail went or the path indicated in this book. The blazes on the Bruce Trail take precedence at all times. Red circles on fence posts or trees indicate no trespassing; these and any posted signs must be obeyed.

Roughly half the walks in this book take you into conservation areas or provincial parks. In these areas, park trails often share the path with the Bruce Trail. Bruce Trail blazes continue in these parks and conservation areas, and so instructions in the text direct you to follow them. The additional, local trail name may also be mentioned. Trails in parks and conservation areas are often signed with both a name and a symbol. Symbols vary from one area to another, but whenever a route leaves the Bruce Trail, it is always referred to by name.

In the few walks that are entirely off the Bruce Trail, our descriptions follow whatever signage is found on the trail.

THE TRAIL USERS' CODE

Many of the trails along the Niagara Escarpment exist only with the generous consent of landowners. If this trail privilege is abused, permission to hike can be revoked. In addition, we have come to realize the importance of such a recreational resource within close proximity to millions of people. Unless we care for the land, we will quickly degrade its riches.

Every hiker is, therefore, requested to know the Trail Users' Code and to practise its ethic:

- **Hike only along marked routes, especially on farmland. Do not take shortcuts.**
- **Do not climb fences; use the stiles.**
- **Respect the privacy of people living along the trail.**
- **Leave the trail cleaner than you found it; carry out all litter.**
- **Fires are not permitted along the trail; if necessary, carry a lightweight stove.**
- **Leave flowers and plants for others to enjoy.**
- **Do not damage live trees or strip off bark.**
- **Keep dogs on a leash, especially on or near farmland.**
- **Leave only your thanks and take nothing but photographs.**

EQUIPMENT FOR THE TRAIL

One of the joys of hiking is that it does not require a lot of money. If you are just beginning, do not spend your hard-earned cash until you decide that you wish to continue. However, if you decide to purchase hiking gear, remember that costly items can be a good investment. Quality gear will work well, prove durable and be a pleasure to use. A cheaper item will often fail under stress.

On a full-day hike, you will want a lightweight day pack, preferably with padded straps. In hot weather, a belt pack or fanny pack can be more comfortable because it allows your back to breathe and also avoids the problem of a stiff neck and sore shoulders. Two hikers could get all their necessary gear in one day pack and one fanny pack.

Each item of equipment you carry in your pack should be as light and as small as possible. When hiking or backpacking, pleasure is inversely proportional to the weight carried; in other words, less weight will mean more fun. Carry a small first-aid kit in a plastic pouch. Essentials are moleskin or molefoam for padding blisters as soon as you feel them, a small pair of scissors, and an elastic bandage for sprains or sore joints. From May to August, carry insect repellent. Probably the most reliable is that with the highest concentration of DEET. Always take your maps and a compass in your pack, and *know how to read both*. Carry a small flashlight with long-life batteries. You will find this so light that you will forget it is there until you need it. A Swiss army knife is the most versatile tool you can carry. Spare bootlaces have many uses, including repairing a broken pack. A good whistle will help get attention in an emergency.

In hot weather, you will need a lot of water. Wide-mouthed screwtop litre-sized plastic bottles are ideal. If you freeze them the night before you hike (leaving room at the top for expansion) and carry them wrapped in a towel to absorb condensation, you can have ice-cold water on the hottest day.

It is a good idea to place the contents of your pack in separate plastic bags to protect them from spills or rain. Similarly, a plastic sandwich box will keep your lunch from being squished.

Rain gear should always be carried, no matter what the weather forecast. It only pours when you forget your rain suit! Gaiters will keep your trouser legs and socks dry and clean in wet, muddy or snowy weather. In hot weather, a wide-brimmed sun hat is better than a cap because it protects your neck and ears. Sunscreen is especially useful to help avoid sunburn or possible sunstroke. In cold weather, a hat and gloves are essential.

Store your hiking gear in your pack. That way you will not forget it when you go hiking. And use your ingenuity. Adapt everyday items for hiking and increase your fun on the trail.

WHAT TO INCLUDE IN YOUR DAY PACK

1. rain suit or waterproof and windproof shell
2. sweater (in case the temperature drops)
3. a change of socks (always take care of your feet)
4. hat (for sun protection or warmth) and gloves
5. water bottle (one litre per person)
6. lunch and some high-energy snacks
7. compass and whistle
8. insect repellent and sunscreen
9. first-aid kit, moleskin and a small pair of scissors
10. map and guidebook
11. small flashlight
12. Swiss army knife
13. spare bootlaces

HOW TO USE THIS BOOK

Each hike description is headed by a summary of the trail length, time required, and grade of hike and also instructions on how to find the trailhead, which maps to use, and where to park.

The time estimate for each walk is obviously an average. Your speed will depend not only on your degree of fitness, but also on your purpose in hiking. Although those interested primarily in physical fitness will want a much faster pace, we assume that part of your attraction to the land is the opportunity to explore the beauties of the escarpment. Therefore, we estimate that the average hiker will be walking at about 2.5 kilometres an hour.

Each of our walks has been classified according to the following ratings:

Easy
Easy-moderate
Moderate
Moderate-strenuous
Strenuous

The classification considers factors such as trail length, elevation change, steepness of slopes, and the condition of the footpath. Each rating is, of course, a generalization, and you should always take into account the particular conditions of the day (temperature, possibility of precipitation, etc.).

An "easy" hike would be comparatively short, over mostly flat or gently rolling terrain, and upon a generally well-constructed path. A "strenuous" hike, in contrast, would be longer, with a lot of ups and downs, frequently over rocky ground.

For an "easy" walk, a good pair of walking shoes will suffice. A family or a novice hiker should begin on these trails before challenging more difficult ones. For a "strenuous" hike, hiking boots are strongly recommended in order to avoid discomfort or injuries. These trails are more remote, and it may be difficult to get emergency help quickly. It is especially important to have some previous hiking experience and to check your equipment before setting out.

Directions to trailheads are based on the Ontario Transportation Map Series, scale 1:250,000, map numbers 2 and 5, published by the Ontario Ministry of Transportation. We recommend these maps because many commercially produced maps of Ontario do not show minor roads. Transportation Maps can be obtained from the Ontario Ministry of Transportation and Communications, 1201 Wilson Avenue, Downsview, Ontario M3M 1J8. Telephone (416) 235-4339.

These maps are also reproduced commercially by MapArt under the titles *West Central Ontario* and *South Central Ontario*. They cost less than the government series and can be purchased at a variety of commercial outlets, including many Canadian Tire stores, larger bookstores and some gas stations. Maps can also be obtained directly from MapArt Corporation, 72 Bloor Street East, Oshawa, Ontario L1H 3M2. Telephone (905) 436-2525.

Where hikes follow the Bruce Trail, we have included the appropriate map reference from the *Guide to the Bruce Trail*. While the *Guide* is by no means essential, for those who already have one, it makes a very useful adjunct to our sketch maps by showing each hike in a larger context. For some hikes, usually where the trail runs through a provincial park or conservation area, a special trail map is available. Again, these are helpful adjuncts; only one hike (Kolapore Uplands) requires the purchase of an additional map.

We hope our trail descriptions speak for themselves. As we go to press, as far as we can tell, they are up-to-date. *But if you find that the trail is different from the way we describe it, remember that the blazes on the trail take precedence over our descriptions.*

We have given some thought about how to respond to queries about accommodation and places to eat. You will notice that on some of the hikes we do recommend specific places. If our selection appears idiosyncratic (to say the least), this is because we feel is it appropriate for us to recommend only those places that at least one of us has visited. We are aware, however, that along the escarpment there are a host of good places that we have not visited and we hope we can steer you towards some of them.

One invaluable booklet is the *Bruce Trail Association Bed and Breakfast Guide*, a small five-dollar publication that lists B & Bs in twenty-five different places along the escarpment. While the entries are not vetted or rated by the Bruce Trail Association in any official way, our own experience has been positive and we have heard only good reports from fellow hikers. Furthermore, some B & Bs will provide a pickup and drop-off service for through hikers. For a wider range of accommodation, dining and recreation options, we hope our list of escarpment tourist organizations and conservation authorities on page 139-140 will prove helpful.

Strolling beside the river, near the Whirlpool, 1926.
– Credit: Ontario Archives AO 1909

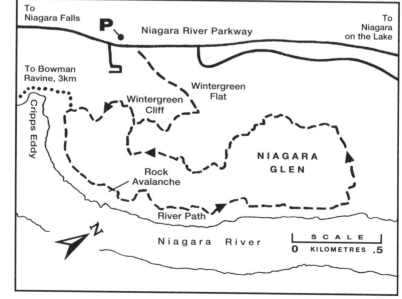

MAP 1

1 Niagara Glen

A Glimpse of Niagara Falls
10,000 Years Ago
The Trails of Niagara Glen

Trail Length: **4 kilometres**

Time: **2 hours, but you can easily spend half a day**

Grade: **Moderate, but the climb back up from the river can be strenuous**

Access: **From the west, take the Queen Elizabeth Way to Highway 405 (Exit 37). Drive east to Niagara River Parkway at Queenston, then south for about 5 kilometres to Niagara Glen Restaurant, on left.**
From Niagara Falls, drive north for about 7 kilometres on River Road (becomes Niagara River Parkway). Niagara Glen is on the right.

Map: **Available at Niagara Glen Restaurant, for a small charge**

Parking: **Free at Niagara Glen area**

For most of the way along the Niagara River between Niagara Falls and Queenston, the towering cliffs of the gorge drop abruptly on both sides to the river's edge. However, for a 1-kilometre section near the midpoint on the Canadian side, the cliffs are set back from the water's edge, making space for a series of fascinating hiking trails totalling over 4 kilometres in length. The trails of Niagara Glen, as this unique area is known, wind through a spectacular wooded terrain in a series of connected stairways, amid a jumble of rocks, which, over thousands of years, have fallen from the cliff face above. The contrast between the wild landscape of the glen with its fascinating record of human and natural history and the tawdry commercialism of the nearby falls area, is quite extraordinary. The glen and its trails provide a remarkable counterpoint to the noise and bustle around the falls. Without a doubt, this is our favourite area along the river.

Like many places along the Niagara Escarpment, this spectacular area owes its existence largely to the ebb and flow of millions of tons of ice. This part of North America was covered with a blanket of heavy ice more than 2 kilometres thick and when it finally melted, ten to thirteen thousand years ago, the removal of the weight led to a slow rebound of the earth's crust. During this crustal or isostatic rebound, as it is known, the land reached a higher level and the flood waters flowing from the melting ice had to find lower-level exits. The formation of Niagara Falls was a result of this process.

Now imagine yourself visiting the Niagara area around twelve thousand years ago—no milling throngs of tourists, only a few native peoples, and the falls a much more modest cascade located at Queenston, about 12 kilometres north of where they are today.

Niagara Glen

1

Over the next four thousand years, rain drainage from a much smaller Lake Erie continued to erode the rock face, forming the gorge we now see. During this time there were three separate small cataracts, about .75 kilometres apart. Then, sometime around eight thousand years ago, as the earth's crust continued to rebound from its release from the confining pressure of ice, the outlet flow from the ancient Great Lakes changed direction. Originally, the lakes drained into the Mississippi river system, but as the land tilted, water began to flow past the Detroit-Windsor area into Lake Erie, greatly increasing the power of the falls and causing the gorge to widen.

This widening began just opposite the present-day site of the Niagara Glen Restaurant and eventually created the glen itself. For the next eight thousand years, the falls continued to cut their way back until they reached their present location. At some point in the far distant future, as the falls continue to erode the river bed southward, they will eventually disappear into Lake Erie.

Today, the 56-kilometre stretch of land that carries the Niagara River from Lake Erie to Lake Ontario has become highly urbanized, but fortunately for us, the riverbank and an adjoining strip of land are publicly owned and have been protected from the worst depredations of industry and development. This protected riverside strip did not come about by accident; it owes its existence, believe it or not, to eighteenth-century British military policy.

After the American Revolutionary War, the Niagara River became the international boundary. As a means of providing adequate security for this boundary, the British decreed that a 66-foot (20-metre) strip of land, called a Military or Chain Reserve (one chain equals 66 feet) be provided along the river so that the government could have direct communications between fortifications and control over waterway landing rights.

That narrow strip remained in the public domain, and one hundred years later, in 1885, the government of Ontario created Queen Victoria Niagara Falls Park, Ontario's first provincial parkland. This was the forerunner of the Niagara Parks Commission, the body that created the continuous river-front parkland we have today.

So, yesterday's military reserve has become today's recreation area. If you want to drive along the river, you can take the Niagara River Parkway. If you are more energetic, try the Niagara Recreation Path, running between the road and the river and reserved for cyclists and walkers. But if you want go back into history to get a sense of the inexorable power of nature, explore the trails of Niagara Glen.

At the roadway level above the glen, you'll find a parking area and the Niagara Glen Restaurant, where snacks, light meals and souvenirs can be purchased. Be sure to pick up a map for a complete description of the glen's 4 kilometres of trails. Now you are ready to begin your exploration.

The first few stone steps take you down to Wintergreen Flat, a pleasant picnic area that was once the old river bed. The water, which was about 8 metres deep, flowed across the flats before dropping over the cliff at the northern end as a waterfall. Cross the picnic grounds to the railing along

The Great Gorge Railway halts opposite the Whirlpool Rapids, 1908.
– Credit: Ontario Archives S18691

the edge of the cliff and take in the spectacular panorama before you.

If you look upriver, in the distance you can see the great cloud of mist rising from the Horseshoe Falls. On the American side, to the left, you get a great view of the huge Robert Moses generating station. Now look straight across and you will notice that the face of the cliff is punctuated by a thin cut-out line about a quarter of the way up from the river's edge. This used to be the Great Gorge Electric Railway, which followed a loop from Niagara Falls, Ontario, via the Honeymoon Bridge to Niagara Falls, New York, then along the American side to Lewiston, where it recrossed the river on the old, low-level Queenston-Lewiston suspension bridge to return to Niagara Falls, Ontario, more or less following the route of today's Niagara River Parkway. During its lifetime, it was a very successful venture. From 1907 until 1932, when it fell victim to the increasing popularity of the automobile and to frequent rock slides, the Great Gorge Electric Railway carried over thirteen million sightseers who came to see the falls' wonders.

The railway isn't the only thing that has disappeared since the 1930s. The famous Honeymoon Bridge collapsed under the pressure of a huge ice buildup in 1938, and the new Rainbow Bridge replaced it in 1942.

Niagara Glen

The Queenston-Lewiston suspension bridge was replaced by the present arch bridge in 1962. And although the Great Gorge railway is long gone, today, part of the line is a hiking trail.

When you look down at the river, you'll see that certain areas have a glasslike surface. This is where the water is moving most quickly. Finally, look down at the woods below you; spread out at your feet is a lush, predominantly deciduous forest. An unusually diverse selection of trees and plants flourishes here. This is because Niagara Glen is part of an area known as Carolinian Canada. The term Carolinian is a sort of nickname that refers to the rich deciduous forests found in a wedge of land between lakes Huron, Erie and Ontario, where particularly mild winters and long, hot summers allow the survival of plants and animals usually found much further south (as far south as the Carolinas; hence Carolinian). Trees such as witch hazel, flowering dogwood, sassafras and tulip tree are among the Carolinian species that are to be found in Niagara Glen.

Now you are ready to descend to the next level of the glen, the Wilson Terrace. For some, it is a rather intimidating drop. A series of stone steps used to lead down the face of the cliff, but they proved too dangerous and have been replaced by a wire-enclosed, open metal staircase about the height of a seven-storey building. This is a very safe and sturdy structure, but if you suffer from even mild vertigo, don't look down; just look straight out and continue to enjoy the wonderful view. And you'll have slow-moving company on the staircase to let you know you aren't the only one who is uncomfortable with heights. Don't forget to look at the face of Wintergreen Cliff as you descend. The hard Queenston limestone was formed from coral sediments of tropic seas about 400 million years ago. Once you get to the bottom, you can relax and take in the jumble of undercut slabs strewn about.

The glen itself remains wild and natural. Although there is more than one descent to the river, a good one to start with is the path to the right along the base of Wintergreen Cliff. The path twists and turns amid huge boulders and tilted layers of limestone. If you look closely at the surface of many of the stones, you will see scores of fossils—tiny starfish and trilobites captured eons ago in the shale. The trilobite was the most advanced creature in the seas 450 million years ago when the trilobite grew to a maximum size of 60 centimetres, but in our shales it is only 5 centimetres long.

About five minutes after leaving the bottom of the stairs, you start to descend on Eddy Path, passing Rattlesnake Ledge on the way. Don't worry; the last rattler was sighted in 1959, and the rattlers were never very vigorous anyway. Then it's down a series of staircases past Lazy Man's Path on the left. After a .5-kilometre walk from your starting point at the metal stairs, you reach the lowest level, Foster Flats, and the river's edge at Cripp's Eddy. This is the exact location of the widening already referred to, created by all of the Great Lakes suddenly using the Niagara River as an outlet.

To the right, a path leads 3 kilometres along the river's edge past Thompson's Point, the northern terminus of the Whirlpool Aero car, to Bowman Ravine. This point marks the end of the buried gorge of St. David's Whirlpool, which, around twenty-three thousand years ago, contained a glacial stream that flowed from this area into a canyon 60 metres deeper than the floor of the modern Lake Ontario.

The indentation of the river on the Canadian side, together with the land configuration on the American side, has created a large whirlpool. The whirlpool's action can be seen quite clearly from the high cliffs on either side of the river.

At Bowman Ravine, the path ascends via a series of stairways and sloping paths to the Niagara Parkway level above. If you come this way, watch the rhythmic surge of water on the wet rocks created by opposing swirls of currents. If you continue along this path, it makes an interesting 5-kilometre loop when combined with the Eddy Path and the Niagara Recreational Path along the top.

If you opt to stay in the glen, take River Path downstream. Where it joins Lazy Man's Path coming down from Eddy Path, you can see the Avalanche of Rocks. These are the eroded fragments of sharp sandstone boulders that tumbled down the river after being eroded by the third (and lowest) falls as it retreated back to join the two upper cataracts near the whirlpool. Here the river is at its narrowest (only 60 metres) and very dangerous. Look, but don't try any rock hopping. A sudden increase in the river flow could leave you stranded; a slip could carry you off for good.

The next step on River Path is Natural Spring, reached by a side trail to a sandstone cliff where a natural spring flows from the rock. Don't drink the water, it may be polluted. We only hope that we can change that in the future.

After 2 kilometres of riverside walking, you emerge on Pebbly Beach, where a hermit named Foster lived off fish from the river and lent his name to Foster Flats. Along the way, you encounter Tiplin Path and Summer House Path, both of which connect to Pot Hole Path, which runs parallel to River and Eddy paths. More about fascinating Pot Hole Path in a moment.

How about plunging deep into the woods again? Follow Lost Path for 1 kilometre as it slowly climbs away from the river along the edge of the old island that separated the two falls of ancient days. You can see the weathering processes at work. Many plants and trees grow out of the avalanched boulders. Pressure created by roots penetrating into the rock causes it to split and disintegrate. Water seeps in and freezes during winter, widening the crack. Just imagine: In only a million years, this weathering process may turn the whole area into a flat plain.

Continue along Lost Path to its junction with Pot Hole Path, which you can follow left for 1 kilometre. Where you meet Tiplin Path coming up from the river, you'll find some of the most fascinating natural features of the glen.

First, the trail descends between two avalanched boulders known as Devil's Arch. As you pass between these boulders, look to the left and you will see a smooth cylindrical hole piercing the boulder wall. This is a pothole formed by water passing over cracks containing sand and pebbles.

As the turbulent water spun these particles over hundreds of years, they scoured out a pot-shaped depression.

Further along is a huge slab of limestone known as Boulder Wall, which fell from the cliff above. A small tree beside the path appears to be propping up a huge boulder. Actually, the boulder was there long before the tree, which grew up beside it, searching for sunlight. It makes you think of those pictures of someone holding up the Leaning Tower of Pisa.

Continue along Pot Hole Path, but keep to the right. You will start to climb back to Wilson Terrace, and as Wintergreen Cliff comes into view through the foliage, you once again meet Eddy Path. From here, it's a short walk to the right back to the base of those stairs. Going up is much less anxiety-provoking, but physically, fairly strenuous, so be sure to keep some energy in reserve for the final ascent.

You can visit Niagara Glen at any time of year. In winter, the stone steps and stairways may be dangerous, but it's worth it to see all that ice building up around the rocks and glinting in the sun, the stark outline of the leafless trees, and a much more open view across the gorge. Visit the glen in spring and you will see the birds returning and the early wild flowers. Autumn, too, is an especially rewarding time for a visit, after the first frost has coloured the leaves. Whenever you choose to go, if you are able to make this trip first thing in the morning (our favourite time), you get a wonderful feeling of seclusion. Guided tours are available throughout much of the year. Check at the restaurant for times.

A hike through the glen is more than worth the effort. Probably no other place in Ontario has such a wealth of variety—the panorama from the top, the excitement of descending into the forest, and the chance to walk beside a rushing river, even to observe a whirlpool—all in one relatively small area.

Urban Ontario's
Green Oasis
The Trails of Dundas Valley

As you drive along the major roads through the Hamilton-Burlington area, you are much more likely to be struck by the human desecration of the environment than by the natural beauty of the landscape. Yet, within five minutes, drive of Ontario's busiest highways lies the Dundas Valley, hilly and wooded, wedged between two white limestone cliffs. Farms and orchards lie scattered among deep ravines and steep hills. Its woodland is home to many rare and sensitive species of plants and animals, and some of its forest areas may never have been logged.

The valley's landscape, distinctive and unusual, has been a long time in the making. Flanked on both north and south sides by 400-million-year-old rocks, the original valley was probably formed long before the onset of the ice ages by a great river that carved a narrow canyon into the escarpment. Later, when much of North America was inundated by ice, the glaciers gouged out a much deeper, broader, U-shaped channel in the Dundas Valley. (The scouring process was so intense that the bedrock in the lower part of the valley now lies more than 100 metres below the level of Lake Ontario.)

When the ice finally withdrew, great amounts of rocky debris were left behind. This in turn was shifted, pummelled and tossed about by the vast volumes of silty water that poured forth from the decaying glaciers. Finally, as the ice diminished and the flow decreased, the debris began to settle and to form the distinctive features that we find today—deep valleys, hills, raised shorelines and moraines—and which give the area its singular charm.

While a lot of the valley has succumbed to urban sprawl, there are still enclaves that remain in an essentially undisturbed condition. And Dundas Valley, like Niagara Glen, is part of Carolinian Canada and supports rare and endangered species of plants, mammals and birds.

Fortunately, the uniqueness of the valley has not gone unnoticed, nor has the need to conserve this precious natural area and to ensure protection for the rarer species. Over a thousand hectares of land have been bought by the Hamilton Region Conservation Authority, and the valley now has four conservation areas.

The area boasts about 40 kilometres of wide, well-maintained walking trails, with signposts clearly marking each intersection. The trails take you through forest, meadow and marsh, across ravines and creeks, and even to the top of the escarpment. Some of the most scenic and challenging hiking in the area is along the Bruce Trail, which joins the Dundas Valley trail system before heading towards the north rim of the escarpment.

The focal point of the entire area is the Dundas Valley Trail Centre. Situated on the former Toronto, Hamilton and Burlington Railway line, it

Dundas Valley

23

2

was built to resemble a Victorian railway station. Open to the public on weekends and holidays, the centre interprets the physiography, history, geology, flora and fauna of the Dundas Valley by mounting displays and special exhibits and conducting nature walks. The centre is an attractive place surrounded by green open spaces and grassy banks. Trail maps are available at a small charge. There is also a snack bar, a picnic pavilion and washrooms.

The Headwaters-Monarch Loop

Trail Length: **8.5 kilometres**

Time: **3 hours**

Grade: **Moderate**

Access: **From Highway 403, take Main Street West (Highway 8) for 4 kilometres. Turn left on Governor's Road. The entrance to the trail centre is about 3 kilometres west.**

Map: **A trail map is available at the trail centre. There is a small charge.**

Parking: **There is a large parking lot at the end of the driveway, near the trail centre.**

You will see from the trail map that you have a lot of options. The loop described here, which gives you a good introduction to the area, takes you through the central area of the valley on the Bruce Trail and back to the trail centre by way of the Hermitage.

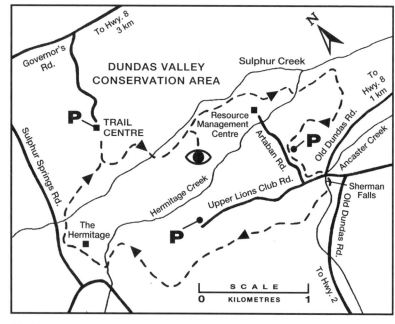

Dundas Valley

From the trail centre, take the Headwaters Trail south across the railway tracks. On the right, you'll find a plaque explaining the geological history of the area. The trail takes you down a slope into a forest of tall trees that form a green canopy overhead. When the sun is shining, dappled patches of light enliven the deep shade.

After about 150 metres, you'll reach a junction. Take the left-hand fork, Sulphur Creek Trail. After a minute or two, the glade widens and you will see some fine hemlock. About 200 metres further on, you will come to another junction; this time take the right-hand fork. This is the Monarch Trail and you will stay on it for 3 kilometres. Follow the path downhill and across Sulphur Creek via a wooden bridge. A wonderful stand of old hemlock shows why this is called Hemlock Grove. The trail continues up the other side of the ravine and, at the top, emerges into much more open country where there are fine views over a gently undulating landscape.

Directly in front of you, though, is the flat Merrick Orchard, its trees planted with military precision. The Orchard Trail goes off to the right, but you stay left on the Monarch Trail, which goes east, along the edge of the Sulphur Creek ravine via a wide, open path edged with bushes, vines and many wildflowers. Obviously, what you find depends on the time of year, but if you are there in late July or early August, we can thoroughly recommend the raspberries. Even if you are no naturalist, you can't help but notice great clumps of goldenrod, Queen Anne's lace, and purple knapweed. The honeysuckle vine runs rampant over everything. And if you take that path in the fall, there is a stand of sumach on the right-hand side that in the sunshine looks almost as if it is ablaze.

If you want to stop for a few minutes, take the short side trail, the Orchard View, which leads off to the right after about 500 metres to the top of a knoll. There is a seat, and you get spectacular views across the orchard to the west and to the north and over the valley to the escarpment rim. On your return to the Monarch Trail, continue east and reenter the forest. Trilliums bloom here in the spring, and later on, ferns form a luxuriant green undergrowth. Herb robert and sweet woodruff are just two of the tiny, shade-loving, woodland flowers that you will glimpse as you pass by.

At the Resource Management Centre, the trail makes a turn to the south, skirting the building. You will pass by a beautiful meadow on your left—a perfect place for a family picnic. Keep a sharp lookout for signs. As the trail enters thick woods again, it forks, so be sure to keep to the left-hand branch, veering east once more. The path leads downhill on a little ridge. The descent becomes steeper, and where the trail makes a little jog to the right, wooden steps take you down the steepest part of the slope. Take care if it is muddy or icy.

At the bottom, a wooden bridge crosses a tributary of Sulphur Creek. First, the trail meanders through cool, deep shade along the bank of the stream. Then it veers slightly to the right, up a hill. Look out for the Monarch Trail sign here.

At the top, you leave the trees behind. Now you are in open country,

Dundas Valley

The Dundas turning basin at the end of the Desjardins Canal, 1896.
– Credit: Ontario Archives Acc 2519 S11917

looking at a rolling landscape that is comfortingly domestic and benign. The trail makes a long curve, first to the south, then west, passing through old farmland and an abandoned orchard. This is slightly higher ground, so you get extensive views on all sides. A strategically placed seat on the top of a little knoll is a good place to take it all in. In late summer and early fall, purple asters and goldenrod surround you with brilliant colour.

At the gravelled drive leading back to the Resource Management Centre, turn left, away from the centre. After 400 metres you will reach Upper Lions Club Road. Turn left again and walk about 250 metres to Old Ancaster-Dundas Road. Keeping to the right side, cross the bridge over Ancaster Creek. Then turn immediately into the woods on your right. This is part of the Bruce Trail and there should be white blazes, but the trail is not well marked here. If you are in doubt, keep to the riverbank and head upstream.

For those who don't know that Sherman Falls exists, it is an astonishing sight. You suddenly find yourself at the bottom of an almost semi-circular rock basin. Directly in front of you, the falls plunge down over three shelves of rock. Pieces of rock face, casualties of the water's relentless force, lie strewn around the foot of the falls. At the sides, small trees and bushes cling precariously to the rock wall. At ground level, much larger trees cast a deep shade that even on the brightest day is barely penetrated by the sun. It is a total contrast to the pretty, domestic scenery you have just left behind. The sound of the water completely blots out the noise of the traffic, so it is easy to believe that you are in a wild, uninhabited place.

After crossing Ancaster Creek on a steel bridge, you will stay on the Bruce Trail for about 2.4 kilometres until it meets the Dundas Valley trails. Follow the white blazes going west (to the right as you stand facing the falls). The trail, which is very rocky at this point, climbs quite steeply through the trees. It can be treacherous underfoot here, so take extra

27

care when the ground is wet or icy. Also, be sure to keep on the main (white-blazed) trail.

You are now on a ridge above the valley. The walk along the ridge, through mixed hardwood forest, is beautiful. In some places, the sun pierces through the trees and bathes the trail in a brief, shimmering burst of light and warmth. At one point you cross a clear, bubbling stream that rushes over the edge of the escarpment, tumbling downwards over the rock in a series of cascades. On your right-hand side, you will see many deep fissures in the rock where water has frozen and expanded, forcing long sections to begin to break away from the edge. Some of the slabs look as if they could tumble down at any moment.

After about 1.8 kilometres, you will pass a trail descending to the right. Be sure to stay left here, on the Bruce Trail. You will find yourself climbing again, through very tall, old trees—oak, maple, hickory, ash, pine and hemlock. After about .6 kilometres the Orchard Trail (one of the Dundas Valley trails) comes in from the right to join the Bruce Trail. You are descending quite quickly now to cross Hermitage Creek.

At the junction just after the creek, the Orchard-Bruce Trail veers right and a trail to the left goes to the Hermitage Gatehouse Museum. If you are interested in history, you might want to explore this particular area. The museum used to be the gatehouse lodge to the Hermitage Estate, built in 1855 by George Leith, the second son of Sir George Alexander William Leith, a Scottish baronet. Although the small stone building and the ruins of the mansion are all that remain, they still have quite a story to tell.

It is probably best to see the ruins first. Then if your imagination has been stirred, you can come back and look at the museum. It is open from Victoria Day to Thanksgiving on a Sunday or a holiday, from 12:00 noon to 6:00 pm.

Carry on down the trail. The Headwaters Trail comes in from the left. Then you join a gravel driveway that leads to the Hermitage ruins. Because the ruins are unsafe, they are fenced off now, so you can no longer explore them at close quarters. Still, if you walk around, with a little imagination you can visualize how it used to be: a lodge guarding the entrance to the estate; a long carriage drive winding through parkland to a gracious two-storey stone house surrounded by fine old trees (some three-hundred-year-old oaks still stand today); horses, cows, and sheep in the meadows; and a cluster of outbuildings at the rear of the property.

The house was used as a summer residence during George Leith's time, but after his death in 1887, the estate began to suffer from neglect. In 1902, his youngest daughter, Alma Dick-Lauder, writer and animal lover, took it over. She was full of great plans to revitalize it, but alas, they all came to nought; the decay continued. The verandah fell off the house, ornamental trees died, the park became overgrown, and Mrs. Dick-Lauder's fondness for animals veered towards the bizarre. All animals, not just cats and dogs, were given the run of the house. Many a tale was told of cows, horses and sheep mingling with uneasy guests taking tea in the reception rooms.

The incongruous household endured until 1934. On October 10, during a luncheon party, fire broke out on the second floor. All efforts to save the building were in vain, and the gracious, if eccentric, life of the Hermitage came to an abrupt end. But Mrs. Dick-Lauder did not leave. With most of the building destroyed, she lived first in a tent, then in a temporary structure built within the shell of the house. She remained there until her death in 1942.

The Hamilton Region Conservation Authority bought part of the estate in 1972, and two years later opened the Gatehouse Museum. There you can see some objects found during an excavation of the cellars in 1974 and a splendid model of the house. Staff are on hand to tell you more about the life and times of the Hermitage and its owners.

After your optional sojourn among the Leiths, pick up the Headwaters-Bruce Trail again. It winds its way through a small pine plantation and then down a steep hill to Sulphur Creek. If you want to look at the Sulphur Springs fountain, turn left after crossing the creek. Cross the parking lot and you will see the fountain on the other side of the road. A plaque commemorates the first fountain, erected in 1850, and the Sulphur Springs Hotel, a popular spot between 1865 and 1900. Around this time, "taking the waters" was a very fashionable pastime and several spa hotels opened in the area. If you've never tried spa water and you are intrepid by nature, now is your chance.

Back at the bridge, follow the trail through the trees to the initial junction, turn left, then retrace your steps 150 metres to the trail centre.

This walk serves as a pleasant introduction and with the aid of the trail map, you will be able to create many more loops for yourself. And don't forget that the Dundas Valley, in addition to its natural beauty, is an area that is rich in history, and one where there are many places, both urban and natural, to explore. The town of Dundas, right in the middle of the valley, is within easy distance of a number of conservation areas and also the Royal Botanical Gardens, so it makes a good base for a short break.

The town is full of history and boasts a particularly fine town hall, completed in 1849. For a brief spell, Dundas was also a busy port at the end of the Desjardins Canal. You can visit the site, now high and dry in the middle of the town. And if you want a historic base from which to explore all these historic sites, try Glenwood, a delightful house built in 1827 overlooking Spencer Creek and now owned by John and Margaret Carey. It has been extended and renovated and is very comfortable, but it still retains its early nineteenth-century charm. The Careys, moreover, give hikers a warm welcome.

Finally, no visit to Dundas would be complete without a visit to Webster's Falls, the spot where Spencer Creek tumbles over the escarpment. In the nineteenth century, Spencer Creek was a fine mill stream that supported many mills, the largest being the Ashbourne Flour Mill, built by Joseph Webster just above the falls that later bore his family's name. Today, the site is a beautiful park, and Webster's Falls, the region's largest waterfall, is dramatic from any angle. You can even descend a staircase into the gorge to get a really close look. A visit to Webster's Falls is a spectacular way to conclude a visit to the Dundas Valley.

Walking Through Paradise
The Trails of the Royal Botanical Gardens

At the mention of botanical gardens, certain places spring immediately to mind—London's Kew Gardens, and Victoria's Butchart Gardens, for instance. But Hamilton, we suspect, is not a name that springs instantly to mind as a leading contender for a worldwide botanical garden award. Some secrets, however, are very well kept, and those of us who have wandered through the magnificent and varied collections of flora at Hamilton's Royal Botanical Gardens, and have hiked along its wooded paths, have discovered a treasure whose worth cannot be overestimated.

The Royal Botanical Gardens has many faces. It combines the function of a university, a museum and an experimental station with extensive and inventive horticultural displays. There are six feature gardens: the Rock Garden; the Laking Garden, with one of North America's major iris collections; the Rose Garden, the RBG's tribute to Canada's Centenary; the Demonstration or Trial Garden, which works out the quirks in new floral stock; the Teaching Garden, nurturing both plants and children; and the Arboretum, which includes the world-famous Katie Osborne Lilac Garden, set in a beautiful natural dell.

But the hiker will especially appreciate the extensive trail system introducing the public to a wide variety of natural habitats and topography. In addition to its cultured gardens, the RBG has 1,007 hectares of land that remain in a natural state, and a variety of trails meander through woodland, marsh, meadow and escarpment slopes.

You may wonder how all this came about. Not surprisingly, the Gardens owe their existence to the actions of many groups and individuals—to the generosity of landowners, sustained efforts by wildlife conservationists and enlightened decisions by sympathetic public officials. But as in the case of many outstanding achievements, there was one individual, a man of great vision and determination who not only provided the creative spark to get things going but also acted as a synthesizer to weave the many separate strands into a whole. And, astonishingly, once it got started, it didn't take all that long. By 1941, when the RBG officially came into being, it had taken less than a quarter of a century to transform an abandoned gravel pit and an area long famous as a wildfowl hunting ground into a permanent sanctuary for wildlife and a renowned horticultural centre.

The story of its metamorphosis is a mixture of fortuity and foresight, with a large pinch of irony. The irony, of course, is that the largest portion of the RBG, the Cootes Paradise Sanctuary, an area of forest, field and marsh at the mouth of the Dundas Valley, was named after an avid wildfowl hunter, Captain Thomas Cootes, a British officer who discovered a hunting paradise there in the 1780s.

As people moved into the area, Cootes Paradise became a very popular hunting ground. Then, during the 1830s, it took on an added role

Sailing through Cootes Paradise in 1904.
– Credit: Ontario Archives Acc 9082 S13052

when the construction of a channel, the Desjardins Canal, allowed ships and goods to sail all the way up to Dundas. For a couple of decades, Cootes Paradise became a significant waterway. Then, in what must have seemed like cruel strokes of fate, its life was blighted. First, there was the continuing problem of silt buildup. Then came the final straw; the Grand Trunk Railroad came to town. These two factors brought about the canal's commercial demise. As William Gillard and Thomas Tooke put it in *The Niagara Escarpment*, "The days of glory were over; Desjardins Canal had become Desjardins Ditch."

After its commercial life ceased, Cootes Paradise's only function was as a source of leisure and pleasure to the fast-growing population. For the remainder of the nineteenth century and until the 1920s, it was a popular spot for hunters, picnickers and boaters.

And that might have been it, were it not for the foresight of a handful of people. From one direction came increasing opposition to hunting in the marsh. Members of the Hamilton Bird Protection Society began to lobby for official protection for the area, and by 1927, they achieved their goal. Cootes Paradise became a crown game preserve. Simultaneously, while the preservation movement was gathering momentum, Thomas B. McQueston, a parks board commissioner, began to articulate his vision of creating a botanical garden that would rival England's renowned Kew Gardens. His dogged determination to acquire land along the shore of Burlington Bay was rewarded in 1930. He received permission to create a rock garden in an ugly abandoned gravel pit at the west end of Burlington Bay. It was quite an undertaking, particularly during the Depression. Hundreds of local men were employed to haul rocks 20 kilometres, by horse and wagon, down from the escarpment. But the result was a masterpiece, and the rock garden they created is still enjoyed by thousands of visitors each year.

That accomplishment really started the ball rolling. In 1931, the parks board acquired a tract of forest and marshland along the lower reaches of Grindstone Creek. More acquisitions followed, and ten years later, the Hendrie Valley Sanctuary, the Rock Garden, and the Cootes Paradise Sanctuary received the official title of Royal Botanical Gardens.

Since then, two smaller areas along the Niagara Escarpment have been acquired: the Rock Chapel Sanctuary, a wilderness area adjacent to Borer's Creek and Borer's Falls, and the Berry Tract, old farmland and escarpment slope, 1.5 kilometres to the east of Rock Chapel.

Among the five separate areas, there are endless walking possibilities to choose from, but you would be well advised to call in first at the RBG Centre on Plains Road West to pick up trail maps for all the areas, and then plan whatever itinerary suits you. The walks described here give you an introduction to each of the areas and allow you to take in some of the feature gardens along the way. None of the walks is difficult.

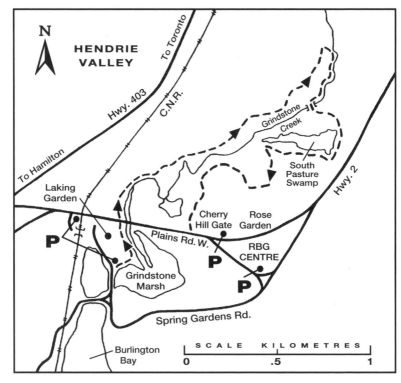

MAP 3A

The Trails of Hendrie Valley Sanctuary

Trail Length: **5.1 kilometres**

Time: **2–3 hours, but add a further hour if you opt to visit the Rock Garden, 1 kilometre west of Hendrie Valley.**

Grade: **Moderate**

Access: **From Highway 403, take Highway 6 north to Plains Road West. Turn right and follow signs to the RBG Centre.**

Map: **A trail map is available at the RBG Centre.**

Parking: **Park either at the RBG Centre parking lot or 100 metres west along Plains Road at the Cherry Hill Gate parking area.**

If your visit is in the summer, you might want to start your day with a tour of the Rose Garden. It is a splendid sight with a wide selection of species roses, old favourites, and pergolas covered with wonderful climbing roses. From the Rose Garden, walk west along Plains Road towards the Laking Garden. If you are there in June or July, go and look at the iris collection; it is one of North America's finest. The range of colours is astonishing. There is also a wonderful selection of tree peonies, herbaceous peonies and perennials of all kinds.

After your tour of the Laking Garden, walk down the hill on the road to the main parking lot. At the bottom of the hill, you will see the Tollhouse Trail leading off to the left. The trail takes you along the edge of Grindstone Marsh, then veers east to follow the north shore of the creek past a number of small wetlands. From here you get a good view up the valley.

With its wooded slopes and flat flood plain, it looks just like any other valley that has been cut by a stream running through it, and indeed, Grindstone Creek has played a major part in shaping the valley. But that isn't the whole story. The slope you can see to the south is a sand bar. It was built by waves that rolled in along the northern shoreline of a large lake that formed when the glaciers were melting around twelve thousand years ago. (Lake Iroquois, as it was called, was a much larger forerunner of the present Lake Ontario.) As the sand bar spread to the southwest, a narrow lagoon formed behind it and submerged the valley. The water, coming as it did from the glacier, was laden with debris, and in the calm conditions of the lagoon, the debris began to sink. The silt and clay deposited by the lagoon waters forms the basis of the soils found in the valley today. But there are variations, too. The soils of the upper flood plain are very rich in nutrients, and you will notice the great profusion of plants as you approach this part of the valley. In contrast, because the south side of the valley is a sand bar, soils here tend to be acidic and low in nutrients, and therefore, only acid-loving plants find it a hospitable environment.

After about 1.5 kilometres, Tollhouse Trail divides. Yellowjacket Trail continues along the north shore, while Brackenbrae veers right to cross

Royal Botanical Gardens

over to the other side of the creek. Take Yellowjacket Trail, which leads you out into the flat lands of the upper flood plain. On your right, you will pass a small pond completely covered in duckweed and algae; if you look closely, you will see the smaller insects walking and sunning themselves on this green blanket! Straight ahead and to your right are some of the larger trees that grow in the sanctuary; tall, with lush foliage, they are impressive guardians of the valley.

After passing a trail that leads off to the right to cross Grindstone Creek, you emerge in Lamb's Hollow, a meadowland area. Many sun-loving plants thrive here. One of the more prominent is the pink touch-me-not, a giant relative of the native touch-me-not. You will come to a point where the trail divides. The left fork leads towards the Lamb's Hollow entrance to Hendrie Valley, but continue on Yellowjacket Trail, which takes you southwest along the left side of Grindstone Creek. The last time we were there, it had been raining heavily and the creek was brown and thickly laden with silt.

When you come to a bridge, turn left to cross the creek. You are now on Brackenbrae Trail. Take the left branch of the trail. You will find yourself entering a forest of trees such as white oak and black cherry. You make a gradual ascent of the west slope, and as you emerge from the trees, on your right, you get a wonderful view of the South Pasture Swamp. It's not a swamp at all, but a pristine pond, and you feel as if it could be miles away from civilization until you spot the notice telling you about Project Paradise, an attempt to restore wildlife to the wetlands. Here, northern pike are being introduced to the pond to bring the carp population under control.

Towards the west end of the pond, Brackenbrae Trail divides; take the right fork. You will pass a small trail leading off to the right, but keep straight on until you meet the Bridle Path. (You join it just short of a bridge that crosses Grindstone Creek.) Turn sharp left. The trail takes you back into forest again and slowly winds its way up the north slope of the valley. After about 1 kilometre, you emerge at Cherry Hill Gate, just west of the Rose Garden on Plains Road.

The Hendrie Valley Sanctuary is very near the Rock Garden. After your hike, if you have time, drive 1 kilometre west on Plains Road to the Rock Garden parking area. An underpass takes you to the garden, where you will see wonderful displays of alpine plants and rock garden species. Wandering through the garden makes a restful and satisfying conclusion to your walk.

The Trails of Cootes Paradise Sanctuary
— South Shore

Trail Length: **10.6 kilometres**

Time: **4–5 hours**

Grade: **Moderate**

Access: **From Highway 403 take Highway 8 (King Street) west. Then, where King Street curves south to Main Street, continue straight ahead on King Street. Turn right to the RBG at Paisley Drive.**

Map: **At the RGB Centre**

Parking: **At the Teaching Garden**

There are some fine walks in the Cootes Paradise Sanctuary, and you can easily spend the best part of a day exploring each of the two shores.

Cootes Paradise has much the same geological history as Hendrie Valley. It, too, lies behind a wave-formed sand bar built across a bay of Lake Iroquois that extended well up the Dundas Valley. The Hamilton Bar is, of course, very prominent; major highways and railways run across it, and the RBG's Rock Garden is built into it.

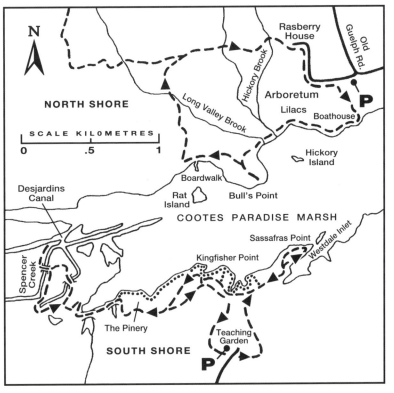

MAP 3B

Royal Botanical Gardens

To explore the south shore, take the Ravine Road Trail, which you'll find to the east of the Teaching Garden. It is a wide multiple-use trail that heads north through a maturing forest of maples and oaks. Then, after crossing a small bridge over Westdale Brook, turn right and follow the Sassafras Trail over ridges and hogbacks through a more open area to Sassafras Point.

From its slightly elevated position, Sassafras Point commands a sweeping view of the north shore of Cootes Paradise and of the Niagara Escarpment curving round from the west, with its many rocky outcrops breaking up the outline. To the east is the dramatic high-level bridge, which was built to carry the railway across the Desjardins Canal where it cut through the sand bar.

As you follow the trail around the side of Westdale Inlet, you'll see lots of waterfowl, but keep a lookout for turtles basking on logs and muskrats, too.

After your circuit of the headland, retrace your steps west for about 300 metres, then take either the South Shore Trail, which hugs the shoreline, or carry straight on for 100 metres to join Arnott's Walk, which follows ridges paralleling the shore of the marsh and takes you through groves of sumach, poplar, black cherry and other hardwoods. It's difficult to know which path to recommend; each one has its own delights. But if forced into a choice, opt for Arnott's Walk. To have your cake and eat it, so to speak, after about 200 metres on Arnott's Walk, take the short side trail down to Kingfisher Point and survey the scene from the vantage point of the Kingfisher Point Observation Platform.

Back on Arnott's Walk, after almost 1 kilometre, you will pass through the Pinery, a grove of giant trees, which includes huge oaks over four hundred years old and majestic specimens of white pine.

Just beyond the Pinery, Arnott's Walk intersects with the Chegwin Trail. If you turn right here, you can descend to the South Shore Trail. At the bottom, turn west and follow the South Shore Trail across two inlets into a weedy, open area. Where the trail splits, take the right fork and cross an abandoned stream channel that was dredged before the Desjardins Canal was built in a none-too-successful attempt to link Dundas with other Lake Ontario settlements. Watch out for poison ivy around here.

Just after crossing the channel, look for Paradise Point Tower on your right. From the top, you get a splendid view of Cootes Paradise. Back on the trail, continue west, cross Spencer Creek, then turn right. After a short walk, you reach the canal itself. With willows leaning over the water's edge, it is reminiscent of a Deep South bayou.

To return to the Teaching Garden, recross Spencer Creek and turn right. When you join up with the other branch of the South Shore Trail, turn right and retrace your steps to the Pinery. After a short stretch on Arnott's Walk, you come to a fork. Take the right-hand path, Ravine Road, and follow it to a second fork. Now take Caleb's Walk, on the right. It runs parallel to an alder swamp as it journeys back to the west side of the Teaching Garden and your starting point.

The Trails of Cootes Paradise Sanctuary
— North Shore

Trail Length: **10.7 kilometres**

Time: **4–5 hours**

Grade: **Moderate**

Access: **From Highway 403, take Highway 6 north. Turn left at York Road, then very shortly left again onto Old Guelph Road. After 0.5 kilometres turn right to enter the RBG at the Arboretum.**

Map: **At the RGB Centre** *(see map on page 35)*

Parking: **At the Arboretum**

Our favourite north shore hike begins on the Captain Cootes Trail. Start near the boathouse south of the nature centre and head west along the shores of the marsh. As you reach the shore, look out towards Hickory Island, the small island not far from the shore. Just to the left you will see posts sticking up out of the marsh. These mark the route of the old Desjardins Canal. By the time you reach Hickory Brook, you will find yourself passing through one of the area's small remnants of Carolinian forest. Here, trees such as sycamore, sassafras and walnut, usually associated with a more southern environment, survive on the sheltered south-facing slopes.

Between Hickory and Long Valley Brooks, there is a low-lying, marshy area, but after you cross over Long Valley Brook, the trail reenters trees and starts to climb once more. A short side trail leads you left to Bull's Point Lookout with its commanding views of the marsh. Soon after you return to the main trail, you encounter another fork. Turn left towards the shore on Marshwalk. When you reach the shore, a boardwalk lets you walk out onto the marsh a little way, taking you through one of the few remaining stands of cattails.

From the shore, Marshwalk heads north to rejoin the Captain Cootes Trail, and after about 100 metres, Captain Cootes Trail veers right to head up the lush Long Valley. You descend into the valley, cross the stream and ascend again to meet the Pinetum Trail, where you turn right. This trail is also the RBG Side Trail, a connecting link of the Bruce Trail that runs between Rasberry House, the Bruce Trail Association headquarters, and the main Bruce Trail about 2.5 kilometres to the north. The blue blazes take you east through the conifers that give Pinetum Trail its name and then out into open country where you get wonderful views over to the south side of the bay. At Rasberry House, follow the driveway south towards the nature interpretive centre and the parking area.

Try to make time to look at some of the tree and shrub collections in the Arboretum. There are marvellous displays of flowering cherries and crabs, magnolias and rhododendrons. If you happen to be there in late spring, you must not miss the Katie Osborne Lilac Garden. With one thousand plants, representing nearly seven hundred varieties, it is probably the largest lilac display in the world. To see it in full bloom is an unforgettable sight!

Royal Botanical Gardens

Rock Chapel Sanctuary and the Berry Tract

Trail Length: **7.5 kilometres**

Time: **3–4 hours**

Grade: **Moderate**

Access: **From Highway 403, take Highway 6 north for 3.5 kilometres to Highway 5. Drive west along Highway 5 for 2 kilometres, then turn left and drive along Rock Chapel Road for about .75 kilometres.**

Map: **At the RBG Centre**

Parking: **In the Rock Chapel Sanctuary parking area**

Lovers of the escarpment, are attracted most to the Rock Chapel area. The walk described here, which combines the Rock Chapel and Berry Tract areas, takes you up to the top of the escarpment, past a sparkling waterfall, along the escarpment edge, through old pasture on its slopes and, finally, down the rock face to view many layers of exposed rock that range in age, some from 420 to 435 million years ago. The route essentially comprises two loops with a connecting trail running between them. You travel over the middle portion twice, but the path affords such stunning views that it's worth the double trip.

From the parking area, pick up the white-blazed Bruce Trail. Follow it back north on Rock Chapel Road and across the bridge over Borer's Creek. Immediately after the bridge, the trail turns south into the Rock Chapel Sanctuary. This is the start of a delightful 1.8-kilometre walk along the escarpment. A few metres along the trail, there is a lookout. If you stop and look back, you get a superb view of Borer's Falls as it tumbles 25 metres down the face of the escarpment. More lookout points follow, and just before the trail swings east, there is a wonderful panoramic view over Cootes Paradise, Hamilton Harbour and the city of Hamilton. You come next to a steep descent of the escarpment, and the trail enters woods. On your right, you will pass the blue-blazed RBG Side Trail, which leads to Rasberry House and the RBG north shore trails. The main Bruce Trail, however, continues east through woods, crosses a deep valley and emerges onto Valley Road. Cross the road and enter an old orchard.

You are now in the Berry Tract, but follow the Bruce Trail for a hundred metres or so to Patterson Road. A few metres to the east is the entrance to the Berry Tract's Thornapple Trail. This 32-hectare property, formerly used for grazing, was bequeathed by Alfred Berry in 1965 with the stipulation that it remain as conservation land in perpetuity. Even today, it seems as if it could be miles from any urban development—one of those many pockets of Southern Ontario that remain in a rural state even though surrounded by urban development.

The Berry Tract is an excellent example of what naturalists call an eco-tone, a place where two or more habitat types meet. In this case, where

Royal Botanical Gardens

mature forest meets overgrown farmland, forest and field species tend to mix and make use of the resources in each other's habitat. This sharing of habitat often leads to an abundance of wildlife in a relatively small area. In this area, deer and racoon are especially profuse.

If you keep to the right on the trail from the entrance off Patterson Road, you soon encounter a large white elm, a lonely survivor of the Dutch elm disease that spread through Ontario in the 1950s and 1960s. Seeing this solitary elm, you cannot help but think of the many thousands of these beautiful trees that once lined Ontario's roads and lanes.

About halfway along the trail, after you have climbed a hill, look closely and you will find evidence of an old road. Not much is known about it, but it was likely used as a temporary rerouting of York Road to the south during the War of 1812. This road would have been out of range of American cannons had their ships entered Hamilton Harbour.

If you are a birder, you will find the Berry Tract walk very rewarding. The profusion of hawthorn gives perfect shelter. This, combined with a rich supply of food, makes the area a desirable place for many species. Rare ones include black-billed cuckoos, orchard orioles and blue-winged warblers.

When you have completed the circuit, retrace your steps back along the Bruce Trail to Borer's Falls. It's not really a chore, and you will probably be surprised at how different the trail seems when you walk in the

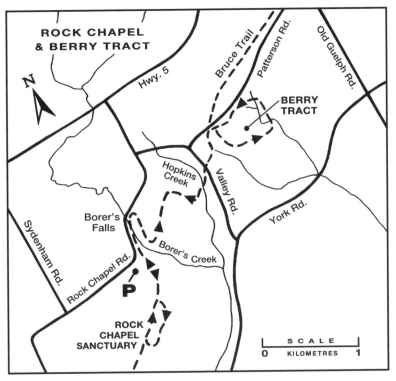

ROCK CHAPEL
& BERRY TRACT

MAP 3C

Royal Botanical Gardens

opposite direction. After you pass the falls, keep on the Bruce Trail. (When you enter the Rock Chapel Sanctuary it becomes known as the Escarpment Trail.) There are a number of fine lookouts as the trail passes along the escarpment edge. A favourite loop, however, is the Armstrong Trail, a short, but rugged, 1-kilometre hike that begins at a notch in the escarpment and, following an old logging road, plunges down through the rubble slopes some 70 metres below the brow.

This is a trail with many sounds and moods, varying from the gentle patter of a spring flowing through the rocks to the rumble of the train that flashes along the railway tracks at the bottom of the slope. The moods vary from dry sunny rock outcrops to a quiet, cool and shady maple forest.

On the initial part of the descent, only hardy plants root in the loose rock of the slope. Woody types such as witch hazel and prickly ash do well; soil is in pockets and very organic. This is a south-facing slope, so spring flowers open first on the "rockery wall."

A few metres farther on, a blue-blazed trail continues straight ahead to an overnight campsite. Keep to the Armstrong Trail, which turns sharp right and soon levels out. The vegetation changes; ferns, trillium and wild ginger are common here. The trail then descends another steep slope, flanked on the right by a beautiful rock wall covered with luxurious pale green moss and occasional ferns such as bracken and maidenhair. At the bottom of the hill, the trail meets the clays and shale that lie under the limestone and sandstone of the escarpment. Surface water runs through the fissured limestone but stops at the shale and seeks an outlet. This explains the many springs that flow across and under the trail.

Just past the ruins of the old maple syrup shanty that burned down in 1976, the trail makes a zigzag turn; follow the signs. The trail leaves the clay soils and again passes through a talus slope composed of dolomite boulders of various sizes.

Next you climb steeply through the geology exhibit. It takes you past millions of years of geological history: layer upon layer of rock, their names making an exotic-sounding roll call. First, reynales give way to irondequoit dolomites. Then come rochester shales, followed by gasport dolomite and ancaster cherts and, finally, the humdrum glacial till of the escarpment top.

At the top, follow the Escarpment Trail east past the maple syrup shanty (if you come this way in March, you can have a maple syrup–pancake breakfast) and onto the left fork that will take you back to the parking area.

The walks described here are simply an introduction to some of the delights that the RBG has to offer. Many more of the hiking trails are equally fascinating and many of the organized events, too. There are morning bird walks, noon-hour nature hikes, cross-country ski outings, wildflower hunts, spring night hikes (to listen to toads and frogs), "owl prowls" and hay rides along the nature trails. The area is an inexhaustible treasure-trove for anyone with a love for nature.

Lakes, Longhouses, Potholes and Ponds
The Trails of Crawford Lake and Hilton Falls

Within a short distance of the large metropolitan areas of Toronto and Hamilton are two conservation areas of exceptional and varied beauty. Each has a wide range of interesting things for people of all ages to see and do. An unusual geological feature makes Crawford Lake a rich storehouse of thousands of years of human and natural history and a fascinating source of information about our past. History is similarly prominent at Hilton Falls, where the remains of an old mill give us a glimpse of early nineteenth-century life. A wide variety of trails in both areas makes them ideal places for family outings or for novice hikers, yet their position on the rugged edge of the escarpment ensures that the more experienced hiker will be equally delighted.

At Robertson's Lime Kilns, below the escarpment cliffs at Kelso. From the 1870s to the 1930s limestone was converted into powdered lime, to be used as a disinfectant and in mortar, plaster and whitewash.
– Credit: Ontario Archives Acc 16856 - 17389

4

Trail Length: **8 kilometres and 1.4 kilometres (Crawford Lake Loop)**

Time: **3 hours and 2 hours (including the Iroquoian Village)**

Grade: **Easy-moderate**

Access: **From Highway 401, take Exit 312 and head south on the Guelph Line for 4 kilometres, or from the Queen Elizabeth Way, take Exit 102 and head north for 18 kilometres. Turn east for a few hundred metres on Steeles Avenue to the conservation area parking lot.**

Map: **Guide to the Bruce Trail: map 11: Kelso**

Parking: **At the Conservation Area. A fee is charged.**

Crawford Lake is a unique ecological time capsule. It is one of the few special lakes where a curious phenomenon known as meromixis occurs. A meromictic lake is so deep for its surface area that the lower levels of water are never disturbed by wind or temperature changes. Without an annual turnover of water, there is little oxygen present in its depths and, therefore, minimal bacterial breakdown. Consequently, at the bottom of the lake, layers of sediment (called varves) build up year by year. Because they remain undisturbed, they provide an accurate record of the human and natural history that has surrounded the lake since its birth.

The lake was formed approximately twelve thousand years ago as water from melting glaciers created vast cavities in the soluble limestone that underlies the area. When these cavities became large enough, the surface material collapsed to form a sink or karst hole. Fed by springs, Crawford Lake developed during the postglacial period into a meromictic lake.

Before you begin to explore, visit the interpretive centre for a general introduction to the area. Exhibits, films and presentations give an overview of Crawford Lake's unique blend of geological, biological and historical resources.

A number of trails begin just south of the centre. A good one to start with is the Crawford Lake Trail, a 1.4-kilometre circuit on an elevated boardwalk that protects the environmentally sensitive shoreline and forest. Much of the route passes rugged cedars and follows ridges with steep drops to the lake below. Interpretive stations at lookout points explain the formation of the lake and its colourful natural and human history. Signs remind you that "Crawford Lake is very sensitive to environmental damage...so please don't swim or misuse the water in any way."

When you stand on the shoreline, it's easy to visualize how Dr. Jock McAndrew, curator of botany with the Royal Ontario Museum, unlocked the mysteries of Crawford Lake. By lowering a weighted tube filled with dry ice to the lake bottom, he was able to retrieve fossilized leaves, twigs, pollen and other debris. Then, by a process similar to counting growth rings to determine the age of a tree, he dated the band of sediment as far back as one thousand years.

An analysis of the pollen content allowed scientists to trace periods of human settlement. Evidence of two major human disturbances emerged, the more recent beginning about 1850 when European settlers were clearing farmland. An earlier disturbance was revealed by the presence of corn pollen in the layers that formed between 1300 and 1510, with the greatest concentration between 1434 and 1459. Since corn pollen is heavy and does not travel far, the conclusion was that an ancient settlement lay within a half kilometre of the lake.

Under the direction of Dr. Bill Finlayson, director of the Museum of Indian Archaeology at the University of Western Ontario in London, a dig in 1973 found evidence of that settlement: six longhouses on a knoll just to the north of the lake. This is the oldest exactly dated pre-European Indian village in Canada. It was occupied by members of the Middleport tribe for about twenty-five years and had a population of perhaps 450 people. They farmed an area of twelve hundred hectares with crops of corn, beans and squash, but shifted their settlement every ten to twenty years when the soil was depleted of nutrients or when firewood became scarce.

In 1982, the Halton Region Conservation Authority began reconstruction of this fifteenth-century village as a way of preserving the natural heritage of the area. Today, a winding palisade surrounds bark-covered longhouses full of animal hides, working tools and bundles of corn. Amid the lingering hint of smoke, three-tiered sleeping platforms line the walls. Each longhouse sheltered an extended family of forty to fifty people.

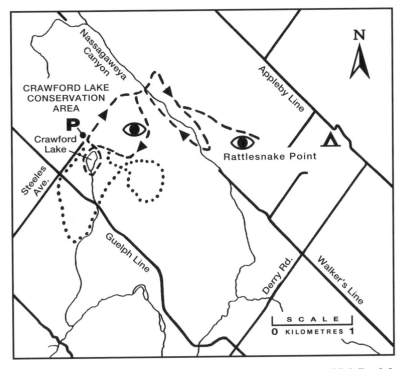

MAP 4A

Crawford Lake & Hilton Falls

An interesting 8-kilometre figure-eight loop begins at the interpretive centre. Turn left at the bottom of the steps and continue along the blue-blazed side trail that follows the Steeles Avenue road allowance. It leads through abandoned fields with some beautiful old white pines and then past farm foundations and stone fences to the edge of Nassagaweya Canyon.

Where the blue-blazed route meets the white blazes of the Bruce Trail, take the path to the left as it heads steeply downhill into the canyon. The escarpment here is separated from the Milton Heights Outlier to the east, cut off by a glacial stream that eroded the limestone and also deposited the sand and gravel exploited by the extensive aggregate pits to the south.

At the bottom of the hill, the main trail heads south (right). Very soon, the blue-blazed Jack Leech-Porter Side Trail turns left into the cedar swamp. Follow this route across a boardwalk and bridge. It is hard to believe in postglacial times that this small stream was responsible for carving out the canyon.

After the steep scramble up the east side of the canyon, turn right on the main trail (blazed white) through oak and pine woods. In a short distance, the trail meets the Rattlesnake Point Side Trail, a 1-kilometre path that leads along the escarpment edge to another Halton Region conservation area. Along the route, there are spectacular views over the canyon. Below, you can see the buffalo pens of a small herd managed by the conservation authority; in the distance, are the cliffs of Mount Nemo. Rattlesnake Point is a mecca for Southern Ontario rock climbers; you can watch them as they inch their way up the vertical faces of the cliffs. Also, you may notice openings in the rock. These lead to crevice caves through which spelunkers can explore the depths of the escarpment.

Return along the path to its intersection with the main trail and descend (to the left) on an old cart track back into the canyon. After crossing the stream, the trail swings right on the Walker's Line road allowance and then scrambles back up the west side of the canyon. At the top, rather than turning right to go back the way you came, turn left and walk along the crest to a lookout point. Here, interpretive displays explain the geological origins of the escarpment and the impact of glaciation.

Leaving the lookout, continue on the main trail for about .5 kilometres until the Woodland Trail turns sharply right, back through the woods to the interpretive centre where you began this figure-eight hike. In the spring, these woods are rich in flowers. Hepaticas, dogtooth violets, mayapple and jack-in-the-pulpit are among the many varieties to be found.

If you wish to go further, there are several options. At the intersection of the Bruce and Woodland trails the Pine Ridge Trail begins. This is a 3-kilometre loop that takes you through rolling woodlands, pine planta-tions and open meadows. From the top of the glacial ridge, you get a panoramic view of surrounding escarpment lands. The loop makes an especially good cross-country ski trail.

You can either take the Woodland Trail back to the parking area or add another 3 kilometres to your hike by continuing southwest along the Bruce Trail. After crossing the Guelph Line, the trail jogs south for a short distance and then turns right into the woods. It goes down a slope into a valley and across a stream. After a short climb on a rock slope, take the blue trail, which joins on the right. This side trail leads out of the woods and through a field on a cart track. It then turns abruptly left to head out to Steeles Avenue, where it follows the road east, crosses Guelph Line and returns you to the parking lot.

Hilton Falls

Trail Length: **9.5 kilometres**

Time: **3.5 hours**

Grade: **Moderate**

Access: **From the east, take Highway 401 to Exit 320 at Milton. Head north on Highway 25 to the first traffic light and turn left on Regional Road 9 and head west for 5 kilometres. Hilton Falls Conservation Area is on your right.**
From the west, take Highway 401 to Exit 312 at Regional Road 1. Just north of the 401, turn right on Regional Road 9 and head east for 3 kilometres. Hilton Falls Conservation Area is on your left.

Map: **Guide to the Bruce Trail: map 11: Kelso**

Parking: **On your right as you enter the conservation area. There is a small fee.**

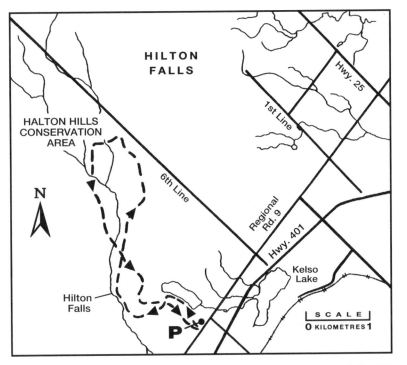

Crawford Lake & Hilton Falls

MAP 4B

From the conservation area's parking lot, look north and you will see the white blazes of the Bruce Trail on the far side of the service road. You will also pass by a Niagara Escarpment Commission display that describes how the landscape was carved out by a large volume of meltwater that flowed through this area during the period of glacial retreat some twelve to fourteen thousand years ago.

Follow the white blazes as the Bruce Trail ascends a small slope and then swings right to the edge of a reservoir. Here, the limestone outcroppings and crevices are fascinating, especially to children. There are wonderful nooks and crannies to explore, but great care must be exercised at all times. There are some large fissures, several of which drop to the bottom of the cliff face.

The trail follows the west side of the large reservoir, which was created to control flooding and regulate the summer flow in the west branch of Sixteen Mile (Oakville) Creek. You soon find yourself passing through lovely cedar woods, but watch your footing through here, especially after a rain. The jumbled rocks underfoot can be very slippery. Just before you reach the head of the reservoir, a blue-blazed side trail swings off to the left in the direction of Hilton Falls. It is a pleasant path through a reforested area with new pine growth and abandoned meadowland. On its way to the falls, the trail crosses and recrosses cross-country trails in the conservation area. The blazing is a bit tricky, but if you are vigilant, you should have no trouble keeping on the blue-blazed trail.

The terrain becomes rougher as you approach the gorge; again, cedars predominate. The trail emerges south of the falls on the rim of the valley, and there are several views of the gorge that are particularly lovely when the trees are suffused with fall colours. From here, the route winds its way north through the cedars. Just south of the falls at the side of the trail, you will see a very large pothole. It is now high and dry, but just after the glaciers had retreated, about twelve thousand years ago, this spot was part of the watercourse that carried the glacial torrents over the escarpment. Rocks lying in a shallow depression were rotated by the swirling waters and gradually drilled a large hole in the bedrock.

Shortly after this, you come to the falls themselves. They cascade over the rock face from a height of about 10 metres. The hard cap-rock at the top has been much slower to erode than the softer layers underneath, and the water that pours over the jutting lip looks like a white veil. The best view is from the gorge below, reached by a flight of steps that lead to a viewing platform halfway down the cliff face.

From here, you get a great view of the semicircular, many-layered rock face. At the edge of the veil of water, lichens and mosses, continuously sprinkled by water trickling down through joints in the rock, maintain their precarious hold. On the far side of the small gorge are the ruins of a

Crawford Lake & Hilton Falls

nineteenth-century mill, now almost totally reclaimed by nature. The mill dates back to 1835 when we think, that Edward Hilton built and operated a sawmill here. In 1857, it was improved by the installation of a fifteen-hundred-pound, twelve-metre wheel made of cast iron. However, in 1863, the mill burned down and the splendid wheel was sold as scrap metal for thirty dollars to pay back taxes. A display at the top of the falls describes its history.

From the falls, the trail winds northward along the upper reaches of the creek, and very soon you begin to see evidence of beavers. The ground becomes very swampy with flooded areas to either side of the trail. But it's nonetheless a beautiful walk through mature trees and past large rocky outcrops. After about 1.5 kilometres, the blue-blazed trail joins a wider gravel path. You pass by many beaver cuttings along the trail, and from the south end of the pond, a lodge is plainly visible and also a small portion of a beaver dam, which extends across the width of the pond.

Beyond the ponds, the trail runs through flatter, more open country, and in places passes through meadow. After about 1.5 kilometres, when the blue-blazes head off towards the 6th Line, keep left and start your homeward journey by following the orange markers of the Beaver Dam Trail round to the south.

First, you pass through a pine plantation. Then the gravel road gives way to a narrower trail that winds through hardwood forest. After about 2 kilometres you cross a creek to complete a loop and rejoin the gravel road again. Turn right and keep following the orange markers south. After a further .75 kilometres, you meet the Hilton Falls Trail. Turn left and follow the yellow markers for 1 kilometre through the woods to the parking area.

While the walks described here give you a good introduction to the Crawford Lake and Hilton Falls conservation areas, there are many other options to choose from, and this is certainly a great place to consider taking a weekend break. A delightful place to stay, perfectly situated on the banks of Sixteen Mile Creek, right beside Kelso Conservation Area, is Winklewood Lane, a beautiful rural property owned by Jack and Nancy Raithby, who give a great welcome to hikers and skiers. In good weather, from the deck overlooking the creek, you can observe geese and deer, but if it's cold, the roaring fire inside will warm your cockles. And the breakfast you get in the morning will keep you going all day.

The Harmony of Opposites
Exploring Scotsdale Farm and Silver Creek

Trail Length: **14 kilometers**

Time: **5 hours**

Grade: **Moderate**

Access: **Take Highway 401 to Exit 328, Trafalgar Road (Regional Road 3). Drive north 14 kilometres until Regional Road 3 veers west to merge for 3 kilometres with Highway 7. When the highways separate, continue north on Regional Road 3. After 1.5 kilometres turn right (east) to enter Scotsdale Farm, and continue along the lane to the parking area near the house.**

Map: ***Guide to the Bruce Trail:*** **map 13: Credit Valley**

Parking: **Free at Scotsdale Farm**

If you enjoy walking through rapidly changing and contrasting landscapes, the trails of Scotsdale Farm and Silver Creek Conservation Area will not disappoint you. Starting and finishing in the tranquil grounds of Scotsdale Farm, the 14-kilometre loop walk described here takes you on an exploration of deep wooded valleys, across swamps, through meadows, alongside tumbled rocks, cracks and crevices, and over a boulder-strewn forest floor. Parts of the trail are quite rugged, others wet, so you would be well advised to be reasonably fit and to wear a pair of good boots. While the walk demands effort and stamina, the hiker will find that it also has its own very satisfying rewards.

The starting place, Scotsdale Farm, was bequeathed to the Ontario Heritage Foundation in 1982 by Stewart and Violet Bennett, owners of the farm for more than forty years. During their stewardship, the farm became noted for its award-winning head of shorthorn cattle and earned an international reputation as an Arabian horse breeding farm. Now managed by the Credit Valley Conservation Authority, the home itself is used as a conference centre, and the property still operates as a working farm, having changed little since the Bennetts left it to the province.

Encircled by tall maples, the modest white clapboard house and its garden of flowers and lawns sit comfortably behind a low, dry-stone wall. Rolling fields, some dotted with grazing cattle, surround the house, and a large barn dominates the farmyard. At the side of the house, a large bell stands ready to summon family, friends and workers in to meals. It is a wonderful place for community get-togethers or a family party. On the beautiful late summer day when we were last there, the grounds were decorated with balloons, men were out on the front lawn playing horseshoes, and children were running about.

With its leisured pace and tranquil setting, Scotsdale seems to epitomize the harmonious co-existence of humans and nature. It's so far removed from today's factory farming and intensive agriculture that you feel "this is the way things were meant to be."

Scotsdale Farm & Silver Creek

5

While the Bruce Trail has crossed the property for several years, a Canada 125 project added a side trail, the 4-kilometre Bennett Heritage Trail, which leaves the main trail and heads east just inside the original entrance to the farm off Trafalgar Road. The Heritage Trail was constructed to celebrate both Canada's 125th birthday and the 25th anniversary of the Bruce Trail Association.

The best place to start the hike is by picking up the blue-blazed trail as it heads east, away from the back of the barn. Just beyond the barn, watch for a short trail that leads left to a pond created by a dam over Snow's Creek, a tributary of Silver Creek. With cedars and weeping willows lining its banks and a resident family of swans, it is an idyllic spot and a wonderful place for children to play.

The trail takes you down a tree-shaded country lane that used to be the rear entry to the property. This old driveway fits all the ideal images of old Ontario farms with a picturesque split-rail fence along one side and a beautiful hardwood bush on the other. You cross the 8th Line, pass through woods for a little way and then emerge into more open countryside. In late summer, the fields are alive with the colours of asters, goldenrod and clover, and if it is warm and sunny, crickets provide a loud choral accompaniment as you pass.

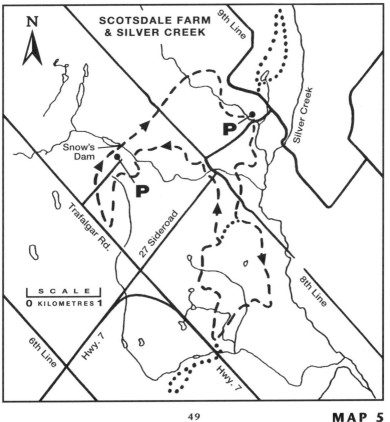

MAP 5

Scotsdale Farm & Silver Creek

5

After about .5 kilometres, the trail drops down slightly to cross Silver Creek. It then makes a wide curve round to the south and descends again to make a second crossing. Now the valley becomes deeper, and you gradually climb, following along the top of an embankment. This is hiking at its best, with the creek valley full of foliage on your left and the open fields of Scotsdale Farm on your right. A stile takes you onto 27 Sideroad, where you briefly turn left to meet the white blazes of the main trail. Then, turn right to follow the blazes south.

First you cross a field; then a stile takes you into trees. As the trail starts to climb, the sound of water below tells you that you are following the line of the creek. Now enlarged by the waters of a second stream, Silver Creek has cut a deep valley, and from the high ridge on its west side, you get the occasional glimpse across to the east rim. After about .5 kilometres, the trail curves round to the west, away from Silver Creek, and begins a gradual descent to Snow's Creek, over increasingly rocky ground.

Snow's Creek descends the escarpment amidst a scene of chaotic yet beautiful disarray. The sides of the creek are strewn with fallen trees, and moss, lichens and tiny ferns cling to the jumble of rocks that clutter the stream bed. The stream, in a hurry to make its descent, skips over its obstacle course in a series of tiny cascades.

As you survey the scene from the wooden bridge over the creek, you can't help but be struck by the total contrast between the stream's wild and unruly course here and its tranquil, well-ordered progress through the pond at Scotsdale Farm, only 2.5 kilometres upstream. Nowhere on the walk will you get a more vivid demonstration of the area's widely diverse moods.

After you cross the creek, the trail continues through cool forest cover and, after about 400 metres, emerges on the 8th Line. Directly opposite, you will see white blazes leading back into trees on the other side of the road. The path through the forest meanders a little, so keep a close lookout for blazes. After about 350 metres, make a left turn onto the blue-blazed Great Esker Side Trail, a 3.6-kilometre trail that makes a loop round to the south.

If you prefer a shorter walk, you can omit this loop and keep on the white-blazed trail.

The Great Esker Side Trail crosses a stile and begins a twisting descent. After about 300 metres, you emerge on a gravel road, and the blue blazes lead you in and out of bush for a very short distance before heading left up an incline into trees.

Although the trail is called the Great Esker Side Trail, this is probably a misnomer. An esker is composed of sand and gravel from inside a glacier, which remains behind as a ridge after the ice melts. While there is no dispute that the formation here is some form of glacial debris, as eskers are not found in this area, the ridge that the trail follows is much more likely to be part of a moraine. Moraines are formed by the accumulation of debris along the edge of a moving glacier and are characteristic of this area.

After about 1 kilometre the trail starts to descend in a series of wide turns into more open, airy woods. Now you start to hear the traffic on

At the turn of the century barn-building was a community affair. Here, the participants pause for a picture during a barn-raising not far from Terra Cotta, circa 1900.
– Credit: Region of Peel Archives

Highway 7 and soon emerge into a large meadow. If you are here in late summer or early fall, you will be totally surrounded by goldenrod. As you approach the road, you come to a hickory tree with a birdhouse attached to it. The yellow blazes pointing left lead across the highway to a 1-kilometre loop that follows the side of a creek. The blue-blazed Great Esker Side Trail veers right and soon makes a sharp right turn, climbing up a steep slope to a ridge overlooking the meadow. In September, you look down on a veritable sea of yellow.

After skirting round the edge of a field, you cross an area of swamp before reentering the woods and starting to climb again. The path is rocky, so be sure to watch your step if it's wet. You cross another swamp —this one is spanned by two sections of boardwalk—and then the trail starts another ascent. After about 300 metres, the terrain flattens out, the path widens, and soon you join up again with the white blazes of the main trail, about .6 kilometres past the point where you left it.

Turn sharp left and follow the path through trees. Soon you will notice small crevices by the side of the path and an increase in the jumble of rocks underfoot. Shortly you will find yourself walking very carefully across a field of large, flattish, moss-covered boulders. Pay particular attention here and don't hurry; it's easy to slip and catch a foot between the rocks, especially if it is wet. This is the debris left behind by the retreating glaciers.

Scotsdale Farm & Silver Creek

Soon you cross 27 Sideroad, and after about 200 metres, you are back in a swamp (Snow's Creek in yet another mood) that looks as if it could be a forest out of the Wizard of Oz. You almost expect the grotesquely shaped cedar trees to start moving and talking. Boardwalks keep your feet dry until you're back on solid ground. As you approach the 8th Line, look for double blazes on a tree and make a sharp left turn. It is easy to go wrong here. Do not cross the stile that leads onto the road. Follow the blazes that take you west just before the road.

The trail passes through a mixture of woods and fields, with great views over rolling countryside to the north. After walking for a few minutes, you encounter an interesting design for a stile. Instead of the usual wooden steps, someone has taken advantage of local material lying around in the field and piled rocks on either side of a split-rail fence. About .5 kilometres after the stile, you make a final crossing of Snow's Creek. Again, it flows through a cedar swamp; this one is very dark and dank but an L-shaped boardwalk at least makes the going easy.

For the next kilometre, the path twists and turns, passing among trees, along the edge of fields and through swampy areas. Then, quite suddenly, the mood of the landscape changes; you enter more mature woods, where tall, graceful trees form a high canopy overhead and the path widens to carriage width. You begin to hear traffic and you realize that you have left the wild country behind. As you approach Trafalgar Road, the white-blazed trail makes a left turn. Keep to the right, following the blue-blazed Bennett Heritage Trail, which goes up a short hill to meet the old main driveway into the farm. The scene before you is idyllic—trees lining the driveway, an old split-rail fence in the foreground, and rising up beyond the fence and the trees, a gentle, green ridge.

Turn right and follow the graceful, tree-lined drive back to the house. Here, the loop ends and the walk that began in the tranquil orderliness of the farmyard comes to an immensely satisfying conclusion. In every sense of the word, you feel you have come full circle.

Another interesting option, especially for families and those people who do not have the strength or stamina to do the long loop, is to visit the Silver Creek Outdoor Education Centre located at the junction of 27 Sideroad and 9th Line. The centre, operated by the Dufferin-Peel Roman Catholic Separate School Board, is used to foster an appreciation of nature. It operates only during the week, but the grounds are always open and contain a number of interesting short side trails, just waiting to be explored. One walk I particularly recommend is the Silver Creek Lookout Trail, which is easily accessible from the centre. If you follow the white blazes north along 9th Line until they head off right into woods, you will come to the blue-blazed Silver Creek Lookout Loop after about 250 metres. The 2.5-kilometre trail takes you up the escarpment and north along its edge. If you want to get a closer look at the escarpment face, there is a ladder that leads down to some of the rock crevices. The path continues north through the woods and rejoins the main trail after about a kilometre. It's a fascinating walk with spectacular views from the top of the escarpment, and it's a great way of ensuring that your visit to Silver Creek Conservation Area ends on a high note.

Down Memory Lane
The Trails of Forks of the Credit Provincial Park

Trail Length: **7 kilometres**

Time: **3 hours**

Grade: **Moderate**

Access: **Turn west off Highway 10 onto Highway 24, about 28 kilometres north of Brampton or 11 kilometres south of Orangeville. Continue west for about 3 kilometres and then turn left (south) on the 2nd Line West. In 2.5 kilometres, on the right side is the entrance to a large Ministry of Natural Resources' parking lot.**

Map: ***Guide to the Bruce Trail:* map 15: Cataract**

Parking: **Use the Ministry of Natural Resources lot.
Respect the No Parking signs along the area roads, both to avoid landowner antagonism and the parking fines which are clearly posted. These regulations are strictly enforced.**

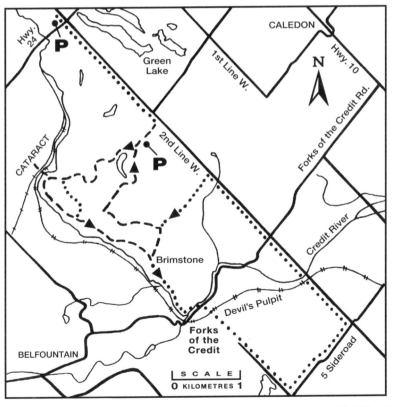

MAP 6

Forks of the Credit

6

The valley of the east branch of the Credit River has long been a haven for family outings. Not only is it rich in geological history and scenic beauty; it is also a fascinating introduction to nineteenth-century rural Ontario development. One hundred years ago, it was bustling with the activities of mills, quarries and railroads. Most of this is now gone, but the curious hiker rambling through the valley will discover the crumbling remains of a bygone era.

At the entrance to the trail system is a large map. Note the Meadow Trail, the Bluff Trail, the Ruins Trail and the Dominion Road Trail, all of which are included in the loop.

Begin with the B trail; it crosses a rolling landscape created by massive deposits left behind by glaciers. As you walk, you will notice circular depressions in the ground; these are called kettles and were created when large chunks of ice broke off from a glacier and slowly melted away. When you reach the hydro line, turn right and follow the sign that reads Waterfalls and Viewing Platform. This takes you past abandoned farm fields marked only by the foundations of old silos, and pine and maple plantations. Soon you will turn left, again following the signs to the edge of the gorge.

Go down the stairs and turn right for a splendid view of the ruins of the dam and millpond. Then follow the trail upstream and across the bridge to the hamlet of Cataract on the west bank.

The tranquillity of present-day Cataract hardly suggests its nineteenth-century activity. In 1879, the main line of the Credit Valley Railroad was completed, and the next year saw the opening of the Elora branch, running along the valley wall. Soon, four passenger trains a day stopped at the junction.

Befitting its status as a railway junction, Cataract's most noteworthy buildings were its hotels. The Horseshoe Inn was the first, dating from before 1870. In 1957, it was rescued by Jack and May Denreyer and lovingly restored. Current innkeepers Rodney and Jennifer Hough completed the transformation, and today, as the Cataract Inn, it is one of Ontario's finest country hotels. Beautifully appointed, it dispenses liberal amounts of wonderful food, old-world charm and genuine friendliness. There are three bedrooms, furnished in traditional style, for those who want to stay overnight. It's a popular place, so book ahead.

A century ago, the most popular hotel in town was the Junction House, a true railroad hotel opposite the depot. For a quarter century, it was the town's centre of activity. Waiting passengers passed the time at its ample bar instead of at the depot waiting room. But in 1907, with the loss of its liquor licence, the hotel languished and was eventually razed. Today, all that is left is a small pile of rubble and a depression in the hillside.

After exploring Cataract, retrace your steps to the river and the base of the stairs. Continue a short distance downstream to the old hydro plant.

First, look at the plaque erected by the Niagara Escarpment Commission to explain the geological history of the Credit River Gorge. Grey sandstone and red shales of the older and underlying formation were deposited in ancient seas over 400 million years ago, and their contact marks the boundary between geological time periods—the older Ordovician and the younger Silurian.

Just beyond you will see the ruins of the old power station.

Development of the area began in the early 1850s with the dreams of Richard Church. For one hundred dollars, he purchased a townsite, and named his hamlet Church's Falls. Before long, a sawmill, a woollen mill and a grist mill were all in operation.

In 1881, after being destroyed by fire, the grist mill was rebuilt. This time it was three storeys high and built from stone hewn from directly beneath the falls. This accounts for the cavelike hollow that exists today under the veil of water. After a second fire in 1885, the mill was sold to John Deagle. He added two more storeys and initiated a lively but short-lived period of innovation and expansion.

With so much competition from other mills along the Credit, Deagle began experimenting with electricity. On November 2, 1899, the first power was generated over five miles of line, and Cataract's streets blossomed with three experimental lights. An inventive genius, Deagle designed an entirely new generator, and business flourished.

Deagle dreamt of expanding his plant. A quarry operator from the Forks was hired to build a steep-pitched concrete-lined tunnel from the millpond to an outlet near Brimstone. The increased drop would have doubled the energy of each cubic foot of water. Over half of the 200-metre tunnel had been constructed when, on April 6, 1912, a massive spring flood wreaked havoc in the valley. The damage was so great that the project was never completed.

This disaster heralded a downturn in the fortunes of the electric company. Within two decades, clearing of forests to the north had lowered the water table, and the resulting water shortages forced the installation of costly diesel motors. The Cataract plant was finally shut down in 1947, and soon the dam was dynamited. Cataract Lake, the millpond and the gem of a village, disintegrated down the valley.

The considerable accomplishment of these hydro pioneers is acknowledged by writer Ralph Beaumont in his book, *Cataract and the Forks of the Credit*.

The Cataract Electric Company was typical of the enterprising nature of pioneer power producers in Ontario. The battle was fought on both the technical and economic fronts...resulting in the Ontario Hydro of today. In close to 50 years of service few interruptions were ever experienced by Cataract power subscribers, an enviable record for a handful of men sweating to keep a plant alive twenty-four hours a day.

From the interpretive platform, unless the trail is posted as being closed, continue downstream beside the wire fence. Take care; in wet weather, the footing along the trail can be treacherous.

There are several superb views back to Church's Falls as the trail joins the route of the old Dominion Road, built in the 1850s to connect Cata-

55

*Scenes of Cataract, painted in 1899 by Chief James Beaver (1846-1925),
a self-taught itinerant painter, skilled carpenter and craftsman, and
travelling showman. Chief Beaver, who was most likely a descendant
of the Cayuga tribe in the Iroquois Confederacy, lived on the
Six Nations reserve near Beavers Corners.*

a) the falls and power station, and b) the junction house and railway.

– Credit: a) Ontario Archives Acc 2748 S778   b) Art Gallery of Peel

ract with the southern part of the valley. It, too, was wiped out in the 1912 flood and never rebuilt. Today, the path is arched with cedars, and on the left are huge slabs of limestone that have tumbled off the scarp. Only the occasional signs of fence posts give evidence of the origins of the path.

The trail climbs up and around a section where flooding washed the clay banks into the gorge, but soon returns to the old road, and the valley opens up. The old gravel track makes for easy hiking. Turn right through the grassy meadow to the banks of the Credit River and keep following the trail beside the water to an attractive picnic area.

If the route downstream from the hydro station to the picnic area is closed, you will have to climb back up the stairs to the bluff edge and turn right. You can follow either the wide path cut through the grasses beside the abandoned farm fields or the more narrow blue-blazed trail at the very edge of the bluff. Several times, this more scenic route will rejoin the Bluff Trail before dipping down again below the crest into the mixed hardwoods of the steep slopes.

This route was part of the original Bruce Trail, officially opened in 1967. If you look closely, you will discover a Hendry stile now almost buried in a tree. Twenty-five years ago this marked a fence line over which hikers had to climb. Today, this part of the trail is another step into history, into that decade of optimism when the Bruce Trail was first being built.

When you meet the white blazes of today's Bruce Trail route, follow them downhill on the old cart track straight to the river. Here, you will find the picnic area mentioned earlier, a perfect spot for a rest, a lunch break or simply to enjoy the beauty of the valley. With the sound of the river blotting out other noises, you can easily believe that you are far from civilization.

The Credit River is one of the most important cold-water fisheries in southern Ontario, especially for brown and brook trout. You will see that special angling regulations are posted in order to protect the river from overfishing; only single barbless hooks and artificial lures can be used, and only one fish over 50 centimetres is permitted for each fisherman.

After your stop at the picnic area, pick up the white blazes of the Bruce Trail as they head downstream. You will pass old apple trees, survivors from the days when the meadow was farmed. Soon you return to the Dominion Road; beside it are foundations of quarry men's cottages from the nineteenth-century operations that supplied the stone for the building of Toronto. The route becomes more heavily wooded, and the white blazes lead back again into the trees before returning to the road near the southern boundary of the park. Just before the gate that marks the end of the park property, look for the blue blazes of the Brimstone Loop Trail; it leads up the scarp edge through the cedars and connects the Dominion Road with an unused portion of 10 Sideroad. To the south is a superb view over the valley, beautiful at all times, but spectacular with the coloured leaves of fall. Across from you are Caledon Mountain and the Devil's Pulpit, and on a clear day, you can see the CN Tower and the financial empires of downtown Toronto.

Forks of the Credit

Soon your route will turn to the left to follow the white blazes of the Bruce Trail as they return to the bluff edge. Be sure to heed the Posted: No Trespassing signs on the right, and stay strictly on the marked route. The trail goes through a grove of sumacs, again a beautiful fall sight, and then passes a reforested area. To avoid private land it twists and drops to a shelf below the escarpment edge. Soon, however, you return to the top of the bluff and before long the A trail comes in on the right. Take this route back across the meadows to the parking lot. During spring and summer, the colour of the wildflowers and the songs of the birds will make a fitting climax to your hike.

The entire area is a rich reservoir of hiking opportunities. To the south of the park boundary, an attractive loop can be created by following the Dominion Road through the hamlet of Brimstone. Many of the small homes date back to the quarry operations of more than a century ago. Follow the white blazes of the Bruce Trail past the Forks of the Credit and then up the Caledon Mountain. This area, known locally as the Devil's Pulpit, is a cedar and birch woodland amid old quarry tailings.

When you reach 5 Sideroad, turn left (northeast) and follow the road for one concession past a huge country estate. Then take the white blazes of the Bruce Trail back to the left along the 2nd Line road allowance. This route will drop below the scarp; continue along the gravel road until you reach 10 Sideroad. Follow it back to Brimstone to complete a loop of approximately 10 kilometres.

To the north of Highway 24 along the 2nd Line road allowance is the blue-blazed Alton Trail. It leads north through the Charles Sauriol Conservation Area and into the Alton Integrated Resource Management Area before arriving at the picturesque nineteenth-century village of Alton. If your group has two cars and can thus avoid a backtrack, this is a delightful hike.

Alton is also the home of one of Ontario's most up-market country hotels, the Millcroft Inn, a converted nineteenth-century woollen mill. There are grand views of the hills, and a picturesque millpond and millrace right at the back door. With wonderful food and elegant surroundings, it's (not surprisingly) very expensive. You probably wouldn't be welcomed ecstatically if you trundled in straight off the hill, knapsack, big boots, mud and all. But if you want to have a look and admire the cascading water, put on a pair of shoes, leave your knapsack in the car and join the merry throng. Drinks in the lounge or afternoon tea (fireside in winter, waterside terrace in summer) can be had for a reasonable price. Of course, if you want to combine vigorous exercise with complete luxury, it is a perfect headquarters for weekend hikes.

The tranquil hamlet of Belfountain around the turn of the century.
– Credit: Ontario Archives OA 10114-18

Our final recommendation is to visit the nearby community of Belfountain and hike the small conservation area that was formerly known as Mack's Park. Its beauty lies in its rich forests and steep limestone faces beside the rushing West Credit River. Hidden in a majestic gorge on the east side of town, the park is a beautiful spot to visit, especially when the fall colours of reds and oranges glorify its sheer hillsides. The creation of an eccentric inventor, it boasts a miniature Niagara Falls, a suspension bridge and a man-made cave with concrete stalactites and stalagmites. It is an unusual place, but another dimension of an area of unique natural beauty that has seen the impact of working hands over the past one hundred and fifty years.

"Over Hill, Over Dale"
The Trails of Hockley Valley
Provincial Park

Trail Length: **13.5 kilometres (long loop) or 5.5 kilometres (short loop)**

Time: **5 hours (long loop) or 2 hours (short loop)**

Grade: **Moderate to strenuous**

Access: **From Highway 10 just north of Orangeville, take the Hockley Road (County Road 7) east for 4 kilometres to the 2nd Line. From Airport Road (County Road 18), 7 kilometres north of Highway 9, take the Hockley Road west for 5 kilometres to the 2nd Line.**

Map: ***Guide to the Bruce Trail:* map 19: Mono Centre**

Parking: **There is good roadside parking on the south side of the Hockley Road at the intersection at the 2nd Line.**

For those hikers who like the challenge of steep hills, the 375-hectare Hockley Valley Provincial Park with its thickly wooded slopes and narrow valleys offers some splendid walks. There is a variety of trails to choose from. The Bruce Trail runs right through the middle and three side trails allow you to explore the park's periphery. Whichever route you choose will take you through a spectacular landscape: magnificent hardwood forest, bush, meadow, and innumerable creeks and bubbling streams.

Although the Hockley Valley cuts back into the Niagara Escarpment, the distinctive dolostone cliffs so prominent in other escarpment valleys are absent here. This is because, in this area, the escarpment is buried under a thick layer of glacial drift, left behind some 15,000 to 13,500 years ago by the retreat of not just one, but four lobes of ice.

Each advancing on Southern Ontario from a different direction, the four lobes met in the Orangeville area. When they split apart, this area was the first land along the escarpment to emerge from the ice. Before they finally melted, the glaciers underwent a period when the rate at which the ice was melting exactly equalled the rate of glacial advance and therefore they came to a standstill. In this stalled state, vast amounts of debris being borne along by the glacier (rather like a conveyor belt) piled up at its front. When the final retreat occurred, the debris was abandoned as drift, which completely covered the escarpment under hummocky moraines, forming a rolling and hilly topography. This in turn has been shaped and reshaped by the region's many rivers, a process that continues today.

Water, in fact, is a dominant feature of the landscape, for this is headwaters country, the place where a number of major river systems—the Grand, the Humber, the Credit and the Nottawasaga—start their sepa-

Hockley Valley

7

rate journeys from sources high in the escarpment moraines. The Hockley Valley, carrying the main branch of the Nottawasaga, is one of the prettiest of the valleys that dissect the escarpment slopes.

The walk described here takes you through hardwood forest, over steep hills, into deep, damp valleys, across numerous creeks, over broad meadows and through marshland. You have two options: one a 5-kilometre loop, the other a more strenuous, but very satisfying 13-kilometre elaborate figure eight. Whatever your choice, remember that the going can be hard at times—a lot of scrambling up and down hills.

The Bruce Trail crosses the Hockley Road at the 2nd Line, so look for the white blazes heading north through trees along a road allowance just west of a private house. The trail climbs steeply for about 300 metres, then divides. The blue-blazed side trail continues straight ahead. You will be returning that way, but for now keep to the white-blazed left fork up a steep slope. You come out into a meadow. If you are walking in spring or early summer, you will be surrounded by flowers: clover, ranunculus, blue flax, speedwell, Jacob's ladder and purple knapweed are just a few of the cheery and colourful inhabitants of the Hockley Valley meadows. Also, you can't fail to notice the bluebird nesting boxes erected by a group of dedicated volunteers, and if it's summertime, you'll see the tenants busily

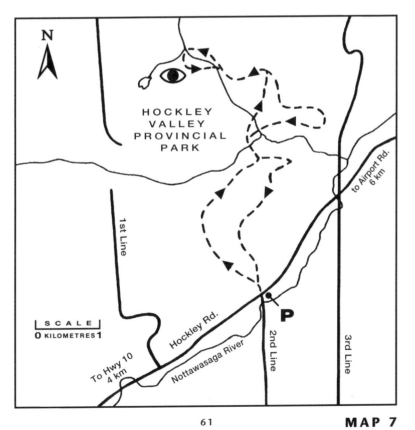

MAP 7

7

Hockley Valley

swooping in and out. As you near the top of the hill, remember to turn around and look at the fine view to the south across the valley.

You descend into a beautiful hardwood forest of maples and beeches and follow an undulating path. Overhead, the trees form a canopy of green, which, on a hot day, gives wonderfully cool shade. In spring, the damp forest floor is studded with trilliums, violets and delicate aquilegias, which give way to a spreading carpet of ferns as summer approaches.

After about 1.5 kilometres, the trail swings round to the right, and you will begin to hear sounds of water. You are on a ridge high above the North Nottawasaga River and about to descend a steep logging road to the valley floor. In winter and early spring, this path can be very icy, so take care. Here, hardwoods have given way to cedar bush interspersed with hemlock and spruce.

The trail runs parallel to the river until it meets the East Loop intersection. This is where you must choose between the short and the long loops. Those who prefer a short, 5-kilometre walk should start the homeward trek here by following the blue blazes of the East Loop, first east, then south, to meet the main trail almost at the starting point. (The description of this part of the hike begins on page 64.)

Those who want to experience the more challenging 13-kilometre hike, turn left at the junction and follow the white-blazed main trail north towards the river. As you approach the place where the river splits into several branches to make its way through the flood plain, the surface underfoot becomes increasingly mushy. You will frequently encounter mud, but be prepared for ice if you are there early in the year; it can make footing very difficult. The actual river crossing is a breeze; three stout wooden bridges take you across to the other bank. Then the trail immediately climbs a very steep slope, ascending in a series of switchbacks. Be sure to stay on the trail. Shortcuts straight up the hill cause erosion.

After another river crossing, you will see the blue-blazed Glen Cross Trail heading off to the right. You will be returning that way, but for now, stick on the main trail, heading north. The undulating terrain continues with several small hills, then a descent into a steep valley with a merry, gurgling stream at the bottom, spanned by a rough plank bridge.

Another climb up the other side brings you to the easiest part of the walk. The ground flattens out, and the trail becomes a broad corridor as it passes through the tall hardwoods. You are likely to meet a fair number of fellow hikers along this stretch. But you should also be prepared for a bizarre, but as far as we know, totally benign, encounter. This section of trail is a favourite haunt of the much-sighted but little-understood Naked Hiker of Hockley Valley; a dark-haired Caucasian male, probably in his forties, who patrols the trail in a totally naked state (not even footwear). His only adornment is a pair of sunglasses, which he seems to don rain or shine. He has been sighted as early in the year as April and as late as the end of October. He is not chatty. When our little group met him he barely (pardon the pun) responded to our polite, if feeble, chorus of "good afternoon." He just gave a cursory nod in our direction as he ambled past. On our part, we were not too swift in gathering together our collective wits to engage him in interesting conversation and so missed the opportunity to find out who, why and where from. Nor have we come across anyone who has. Among those who have reported their sightings, almost all confess to being struck dumb by the encounter. Reactions are predictably mixed: some have felt quite alarmed, but most express a mixture of amazement and amusement; indeed, some even express concern, particularly for his bare feet, and for the danger of UV damage to normally unexposed areas of skin.

Anyhow, whether you meet him or not, it's probably best to know he exists so that you aren't too taken aback if he does wander into view.

After the flat section, follow the white blazes up a long, steep hill until you come to an intersection where the blue-blazed Snell Loop goes off to the left. If you have a little energy to spare, the walk around this loop will take you through some of the most beautiful scenery on this section of the trail. If you are beginning to flag a little, 100 metres along the main trail you will find the Glen Cross Loop and the start of the homeward journey. (Omitting the Snell Loop will shorten the hike by about 3 kilometres.)

Those who opt to do the Snell Loop will find themselves walking through stately hardwoods on a gradual descent down a ridge to a river valley. After about .8 kilometres, the trail forks; take the right-hand fork (you will use the other for your return), leading uphill. You climb out of the valley again past stands of hemlock, white birch and beech trees. At the top, you come out into open country and an utterly peaceful landscape. A wooded ridge forms the background to meadows, dotted here and there with cedars, two tranquil ponds and a very picturesque old split-rail fence. Flowers abound, but in mid-July the meadow is dominated by great clumps of wild indigo that form brilliant yellow patches at your feet. This is a lovely spot for lunch.

The trail continues west along the edge of the woods, then makes a sharp turn to the left at double blue blazes. (The turn is easy to miss, so keep a sharp lookout for the Bruce Trail diamond and the blazes on a post.) You pass through sumac-dotted fields until once more you reenter the forest. The trail forks once more, and this time you take the left branch. At the river, the trail heads first downstream, then across the river to join the original trail and retrace the path back to the main trail.

Continue north for about 100 metres until you reach the Glen Cross Loop leading off to the right. The blue blazes lead you south, then east. After you descend into a large meadow, the path crosses a pretty stream. The route is a bit tricky here, so keep a sharp lookout for blazes that lead you up a steep hill into trees once more. As you come out of the trees, you get some great views to the south over the Hockley Valley. On a calm, clear summer's day, you will look down on an idyllic rural scene. Directly ahead is the south rim of the valley, its slopes uniformly wooded except for the light green alleyways of the Hockley Valley ski trails, dressed in their summer garb. Below, a ribbon of road carries silent, toy-town cars through the tiny riverside hamlets of Glen Cross and Woodside.

The trail leads you down a hill, then through another large meadow, past a large stand of sumacs—spectacular in their fiery autumn finery. After you reenter the trees, look out carefully for blazes and stay on the

63

Never an easy job: a road construction crew at work in 1905.
– Credit: Region of Peel Archives N110.8

blue-blazed trail. You will cross over yet another stream, then travel along a high, wooded ridge, which meets up again with the main trail.

You retrace your steps for about 1 kilometre, recrossing the bridges over the river and returning through the cedars to the intersection with the East Loop.

Now you leave the main trail, turning east to follow the blue blazes. You will find yourself in a wide, very wet corridor, with a rivulet running down the centre and the trail running parallel on the right-hand side on slightly elevated ground. After about 400 metres, it veers to the right up a short hill. At the top, you meet a rail fence and bear right, following the fence line until you reach a stile that takes you into a meadow. The blazes are very difficult to see, but bear right, skirting round the periphery of the meadow, and when you round the corner, you will see blue-blazed apple trees stretching in a line directly in front of you. To your left is beautiful rolling countryside; bird boxes dot the slopes and, in summer, Queen Anne's lace and large daisies delight your eye as they wave their heads among the tall grasses.

The trail takes you past a grove of butternut trees, up an incline, and into a very pretty stand of young cedars. When you emerge you will see woodland on your left and a large field stretching ahead and to your right. Walk straight up the field, keeping the tree line on your left. At the top, a stile takes you over a fence into woods. Turn sharp left and follow an undulating trail through the forest for about a kilometre until you rejoin the main trail just above the Hockley Road.

After your walk, if you have time, visit Hockley Village. The 7-kilometre drive east along the Hockley Road alongside the river is very pleasant and takes you along one of the oldest thoroughfares in Ontario. There is speculation that the escarpment's larger valleys, those that cut deep notches into its face, could well have been routes through which caribou migrated and that, wherever the caribou moved, early man followed close behind. In any event, the Hockley Valley became an important Indian trail and later was one of the main routes to bring settlers into the area.

It wasn't an easy journey, though; the river saw to that. When the first road was built in 1876, there was so much swamp and so many streams to cross that in many sections the road builders had to lay huge cedar logs to literally carry the route over the wetlands. But the work was well done; those logs lasted for ninety years.

The river, however, did not always consent to be so tidily subdued. One of the saddest and most vividly remembered river disasters occurred along the Hockley Road. In *Into the High Country* Adelaide Leitch tells the tale of William and Bella Wisdom, residents of the valley who, in May 1908, were swept away by a flash flood as they took shelter from a rainstorm under a bridge. The raging torrent piled up trees and debris along its course and, at the 7th Line, raised the Hockley Road by a height of over six feet. The Wisdoms' eight children were orphaned by the storm.

The Hockley Road looks benign enough now, but as you pass the 7th Line, you may feel the urge to hurry along to Hockley. Happily, it still manages to retain a tranquil, old-world charm. The hub of the village is the Driveshed, built in 1837 as a hotel and general store. Today, you can buy good breads, home-baked goods and locally grown food there, and also somewhat up-market gifts, art and craft items, and antiques. You can get food and lodging too. Lunch and traditional teas are served in the Hockley House Tea Room (beside a blazing fire in winter), and upstairs there are four bedrooms, all with pine floors and antique furniture. Reservations are a must for accommodation. Close by, a number of smaller buildings make a sort of village square, where you'll find a bookshop, a craft store, an art and carving gallery, an antiques barn and a second-hand shop. Just down the road, Hockley's Country Inn is another pleasant place for lunch or dinner (in summer on the patio, in winter by the fire; it's licensed too). It also has three charming bedrooms for overnight guests. But again, you must book ahead.

For those who would like to spend two or three days exploring the escarpment, Hockley Village is the perfect place to stay—tranquil yet very hospitable; rural yet easy to reach.

My Heart's in the Highlands
The Trails of Mono Cliffs
Provincial Park

Trail Length: **11 kilometres or 3.5 kilometres (alternative trail)**

Time: **4.5 hours or 1.5 hours (alternative trail)**

Grade: **Moderate**

Access: **Turn east off Highway 10 on 15 Sideroad (Regional Road 8) at Camilla, 9 kilometres north of Orangeville. After 3.5 kilometres, take the 2nd Line north to Mono Centre. Or, turn west off Airport Road 12.5 kilometres north of Highway 9 onto Regional Road 8 to Mono Centre.**

Map: ***Guide to the Bruce Trail:* map 19: Mono Centre. A brochure containing a trail map can sometimes be found in the boxes in the parking areas, or it can be obtained from the Ministry of Natural Resources, Queen's Park, Toronto, Ontario M7A 1W3. Telephone (416) 314-2000**

Parking: **The rather poorly marked south entrance to Mono Cliffs Provincial Park parking lot is about 200 metres east of Mono Centre on the north side of the road.**

There are a number of theories about the origin of the name Mono. The most persuasive of these links it to the first settlers of the area, Gaelic-speaking Scots. Mono, it is suggested, came from the Gaelic word *monadh,* a hill, and was chosen perhaps because the landscape was reminiscent of the Scottish Highlands.

It is very different today, of course. The thick forest has long gone, and a network of roads, for the most part passable all year round, follow concession lines that were painstakingly delineated a century and a half ago. Yet in spite of these changes, as you approach Mono Centre, you begin to get some sense of the area's highland nature and to see why it might have struck a chord of recognition in the mind of a homesick settler. If you are coming from the south, once you enter Dufferin County, long referred to as "the roof of Ontario," the countryside takes on a different aspect; it is wilder and higher and steeper than the flat or gently undulating lands nearer Lake Ontario. And you are surrounded by hills.

You might also notice the absence of the Niagara Escarpment, and those interested in geography might wonder where it has gone. In fact, it lies buried under a thick mantle of glacial rubble, and you will barely catch a glimpse of it until you enter Mono Cliffs Provincial Park.

But when you get there, what a glimpse! In this small, 750-hectare space, the escarpment seems to have gathered together its most stunning features to put on a show of unsurpassed drama and loveliness; but rather like the opera singer who knows that overexposure destroys the magic, its appearance is glorious, yet very brief. North of the park, it disappears underground once more.

Variety is the keyword. Assembled before you, just waiting to be explored, are deeply fissured, vertical dolostone cliffs and two isolated rock outliers, a deep glacial spillway, a swamp, streams, ponds and a kettle lake—scenery that plays host to a diverse and exuberant cast of characters from both plant and animal worlds. There are 450 plant species, some of them very rare. In particular, there are several species of ferns, including the walking fern, hart's tongue fern and grape ferns, which make the area a botanist's delight.

The Bruce Trail passes through and, within the park, there are a number of trails of varying lengths and degrees of difficulty. The 11-kilometre walk described here allows you to explore many of the park's most dramatic features. Starting where the Bruce Trail heads north from the parking area, it takes you between the escarpment and the south outlier, out onto the glacial spillway, up to the top of the escarpment, then west and south to skirt McCarston's lake. The return takes you along the cliff edge, down the escarpment, across wetland and back to the starting point.

As you pick up the white-blazed Bruce Trail heading north from the parking lot, you find yourself on a wide track lined with cedar, pine, spruce

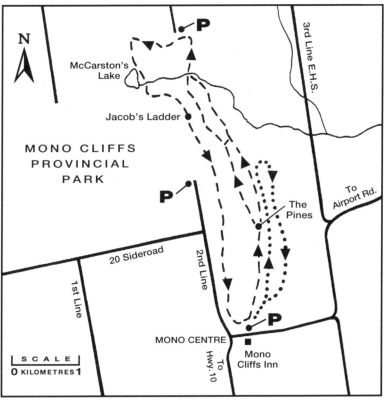

Mono Cliffs

MAP 8

8

and balsam. The scent hanging in the air after a spring shower is wonderful. High cliffs on either side give you the feeling that you are walking through a canyon. On your right is the south outlier, a great mass of limestone that has become detached from the main escarpment. Outliers are formed when glacial ice erodes an area of weakened bed-rock. The erosion was later intensified by swirling waters from decaying glaciers that washed away the overlying material and created a deep channel, the Violet Hill Spillway, which carried sediment-laden run-off southward towards what is now Orangeville.

After .85 kilometres, you come to the Pines, a pretty clearing dotted with picnic tables. If you look up you may see some large birds wheeling and soaring high above you. They are turkey vultures, and the hot air currents generated by closely spaced high cliffs make the canyon a popular place for their aerobatics.

At this point, you have a choice of two interconnecting and almost parallel trails; both follow the spillway and each gives you a good look at the base of the cliffs. To the right, the Spillway Trail takes you nearer the outlier, while the Bruce Trail, to the left, takes you towards the base of the escarpment. Both trails pass through woods that in springtime are carpeted with trilliums.

They come out into open country close to two ponds. The ground is pretty marshy here and you'll see lots of evidence of beaver activity. You can cross from one trail to the other at this point if you wish.

The Bruce Trail stays on the west side of the ponds, but the white blazes are a little haphazard here, so you need to be vigilant. A wide trail crosses the area between the ponds, but if you want to remain on the Bruce Trail, take the narrower, left fork, which enters a wet, lightly wooded area where there are lots of birch. About .75 kilometres further on, there is another tricky spot that is easy to miss. The Bruce Trail veers sharply to the right up a hill, through cedars and birch, to bring you out on the top of a small knoll facing a very pretty stand of cedars. The view from this point is very fine. To the northeast, you can see the cliffs of the north outlier, and to the southeast, you look down over the rolling lands of the glacial spillway.

If you opt to take the Spillway Trail, after the ponds, you pass over old farmland. In the spring, the apple blossom makes this a particularly attractive walk. (Later in the year, the apples are much sought after by white-tailed deer.) After about .75 kilometres, look to your right and you will see the remains of an old homestead, one of several to be found in the park. If you make a brief detour across marshy ground, you can get a closer look. Parts of the four walls are still standing, and you can see very clearly how they were constructed. Stones and small boulders must have been painstaking gathered together, piled up and set in mortar. Fruit trees and lilac grow near to the ruins, and the remains of an outbuilding stand close by.

If you happen to be in the park on a still, balmy day, the bucolic charm of the scene gives these old homesteads a romantic air. But if you happen to be there in a snowstorm on a bitingly cold day in March, as you stand there, struggling to remain upright, you can't help but wonder what sort of person would have the audacity to clear the forest, build a homestead and attempt to carve a livelihood out of such a wild and inhospitable place. How many times did a late frost decimate the apple blossoms or the newly sprung wheat? How often did livestock fall prey to marauding wolves? How many settlers succumbed to despair? From contemporary accounts, quite a number. The area was noted for its harshness and only certain people survived. In a survey of early settlers in 1825, Robert Weaver observed, "Not one in five succeeds, but the Scotch and the North of Ireland people, accustomed to hard work and spare living, seldom fail."

After this brief encounter with the past, follow the Spillway Trail for about 100 metres until it meets the Bruce Trail. Then follow the white blazes of the Bruce Trail towards the escarpment. A long climb takes you to the top. The area to your left, part of a natural regeneration zone, is posted off limits, but as you climb, you will catch glimpses of the rock face. To your right, the views over the spillway get better and better as you gain height. At the top, the trail swings west through open country, and after passing the northern entrance to the park on the 2nd Line road allowance, it takes you to a splendid lookout—one of the highest points in the park, a grassy knoll dotted with small outcrops of rock. It is a very popular place for picnics and it's easy to see why. Immediately below you are the treetops of the deciduous forest; beyond them, cliffs, the deep spillway and a clear view of the rolling hills around Orangeville. Incidentally, this is about the midpoint of the walk, so it's an ideal place to take a break.

From the lookout point, the trail veers northwest, passes through a hawthorn savanna area, then enters a beautiful hardwood forest. These woods have an airy feel to them. The branches of the tall trees form a high canopy overhead, and in sunshine their wind-stirred leaves create ever-changing patterns of light and shade. On the forest floor, verdant ferns flourish. In the spring, you'll see both red and white trillium and, in the cool shade around moss-covered rocks, violets and the graceful and delicate aquilegia thrive. You may notice that many of the trees hereabouts are peppered with large holes—the work of the pileated woodpecker.

At a T-junction, the Bruce Trail meets the blue-blazed McCarston Lake Trail. Here again you have a choice; either branch of the side trail will take you back to your starting point. We recommend that you take the left branch as it allows you to look at the lake and, further on, to explore the escarpment face.

McCarston's Lake first comes into view through the trees on your right, and soon you will find yourself on a raised ledge, looking down on serene waters surrounded by birch and poplar. The lake, the only natural lake in Mono Township, is what is known as a kettle lake, and was formed thirteen to fourteen thousand years ago by the gradual melting of a huge, buried piece of ice that had been left behind by a retreating glacier.

Mono Cliffs

Mono Centre at the turn of the century.
– Credit: Dufferin County Museum

The blue blazes take you out of the trees to skirt alongside hummocky, derelict farm fields, then east towards the escarpment edge. A cart track running along the 2nd Line road allowance makes things a bit tricky here. Be sure to follow the blue blazes, which take you east of the cart track to the area known as Jacob's Ladder. (If you find yourself at a junction with the Cliff Top Trail, you have missed the way, but don't worry, a left turn onto the Cliff Top Trail will bring you to Jacob's Ladder after about 150 metres.) Here, a steel staircase leading down the escarpment gives you a spectacular close-up of the 30-metre high cliffs.

The cliff face contains the fossilized remains of marine creatures that swam in an inland sea, which covered the area 400 million years ago. As you descend, you will see stunted cedars, now known to be up to eight hundred years old, clinging to fissures in the rock. In places where large sections of bedrock have slumped away from the face, there are deep and narrow crevice caves. Put your hand or face to the entrance and you will feel a draft of cold air, even on the hottest day. Cold microclimates in the caves keep ice and snow intact into June and July. The base of the cliff is strewn with piles of rocky debris known as talus, the result of water freezing in joints and cracks and causing chunks of rock to break off the cliff face. You will notice ferns and mosses growing here, many of them rare.

Continuing south from Jacob's Ladder, you take the Cliff Top Trail, which approaches on the left. Be sure to heed the signs and stay well back from the cliff face.

After about .5 kilometres, the Cliff Top Trail crosses over the E-W Carriage Trail, a short path that leads from the 2nd Line to the Bruce Trail. By turning left, you can make this an alternative route back to the parking area. A staircase has been built down the escarpment, and a number of panels explain the geology, history, flora and fauna of the area. If you opt to stay on the Cliff Top Trail, you reach open country just after the crossing. You are back from the escarpment edge now, but still on high ground and there are wonderful views of the cliffs to the east. You pass through open grassland planted with stands of pine and dotted here and there with ash, cherry and apple trees. After about 1.5 kilometres, you meet the trees and the cliff top once more and begin your descent. The trail is steep and rocky; take care if it is wet or icy. Water seepage at the bottom means that you will invariably encounter mud but remember, as you squelch grumblingly through it, that many of the park's rare and shallow-rooted plant species thrive in this area. The trail takes you on through marshland, between two ponds where you may see mallards, black ducks and even the great blue heron.

About 100 metres past the ponds, your 11-kilometre loop is completed where the Cliff Top and Bruce trails meet, just before the entrance to the parking area.

If you feel you haven't had quite enough exercise, you can add another 3.5 kilometres to your walk by exploring the top of the south outlier. This short loop, which gives you wonderful views, particularly to the east and south, is delightful both by itself and as an adjunct to another walk.

Join the white-blazed Bruce Trail where it makes a sharp turn up a hill just northeast of the parking area. There is a short, steep climb through cedars to the top of the outlier. At the top, stay to the left and take the blue-blazed side trail, which runs north along the west rim. This is a shady walk, cool even on the hottest day, first through conifers, then mixed forest. You get the occasional glimpse of the escarpment cliffs on the other side of the canyon, but as the cliff edge where you are walking is crumbly, you should be careful to stay on the trail. Be patient, because after about a kilometre you'll come to a good lookout point that gives you fine views of the opposite cliff face and the rolling countryside to the northeast.

As you approach the north end of the outlier, the path begins a gradual descent and veers east, then south through tall trees, mostly maple, birch and beech. In the spring the ground is covered with trilliums and both white and purple violets. On the east side of the outlier the large trees gradually give way to smaller stands of young birch and maple, interspersed with apple, staghorn sumac, hawthorn and ash. You come out into open country at a very pretty lookout—a grass-covered hillside—and you find yourself above a large stand of sumac. Beyond, the ground falls away quite sharply to the east and you get wonderful views over the Hockley Valley.

The trail continues south through old pastures that are now being taken over by hawthorn and sumac. Near a hydro line, you will meet the white blazes of the main Bruce Trail coming in on your left. Blue and white blazes guide you past a number of bluebird nesting boxes to complete the loop. Retrace your steps down to the parking area.

This walk is lovely at any time of the year; carpeted with flowers in spring, cool in summer and ablaze with colour in the fall. But the best we have ever seen it was in January on a day following an ice storm. The air was still and it was very cold, but the sun shone from a cloudless sky and every branch, every twig and every blade of grass was encased in a shimmering coat of ice. The only sound that broke the silence was the creaking of hard-frozen snow under our boots, and the view, when we got to the east side of the outlier, seemed to go on forever.

Out of the sun, the cold was so intense that we fairly scuttled down the final slope. By that time only one thing was on our minds; hot soup at the Mono Cliffs Inn.

Mono Centre was never very large, but during the second half of the nineteenth century, it was the lively hub of Mono Township, with a general store, a post office, a hotel and a flour mill. By 1888, the eighty-eight residents could get most things they needed right there in the village. A carpenter, a weaver, a shoemaker and a carriage maker catered to their daily needs, while the blacksmith saw to it that the horses were kept in good fettle. There was even an insurance agent.

But the site under the brow of the escarpment, picturesque as it may have been, was a disadvantage. Mono Centre was difficult to reach; road and rail communication was so much more easily established in other places. So inevitably, as the more easily accessible towns developed, commercial activity in Mono Centre declined.

The 140-year old Mono Cliffs Inn is the present-day hub of the hamlet. It has been imaginatively restored by owners Carol and Mike Hall. (She is Australian, and he is Scottish but sounds English.) On the main floor there is a restaurant—beams, lots of wood and a stencilled floor—and downstairs, a pub, Peter's Cellar, that looks and feels like a real pub (more beams, thick, white-washed stone walls and a stove). Both pub food and more formal meals are superb, so not surprisingly, it is a very popular place. Hikers are welcome provided there are not too many of them at one time. Carol says quite bluntly, "We can't cope with a bus load." But if your group is small, you'll find it's a great posthike watering hole at any time of year.

If you feel like browsing, there is a little enclave of interesting shops and galleries across the inn's yard. But if you have a little time and you are interested in history, walk or drive up to the Burns' Cemetery. It's on a hill just north of the village on the 2nd Line and it has been there since 1835.

The first settlers in Mono Centre were the Turnbulls, who arrived in 1822 from Scotland, via New York State. More Scottish Turnbulls came to join them. Other prominent Scottish settlers, Alex and Maggie Laidlaw, donated the land for the cemetery.

The lettering on some of the very early headstones has been all but obliterated by 150 years of exposure, but you can see that Scottish and Irish names predominate. Some headstones tell you where the owners of the names came from; for instance, there are Neils from Aberdeen and Millars from Ireland. You can't help but notice that 150 years ago, people died young; Alexander Neil, who died at 34, and Charles McCutcheon, at 27, are perhaps a testament to the hard life of the early settler. Later inscriptions tell you that towards the end of the century, people began to survive longer, and as you wander around you realize that a small group of family names such as Turnbull, Laidlaw, Patterson and Muirhead continue on, generation after generation. And you notice that they are a tenacious lot, some members surviving into their nineties.

When you leave the cemetery, look at the notice describing its history. At the end, the name of the current secretary-treasurer appears, Jean Turnbull, whose family just happens to live in a home on the lot that was cleared by the first Turnbulls in 1822. You can learn a lot about a place from its cemetery, and from this one, you get a strong sense of the character of this little community and, above all, its continuity. Mono Centre, you feel, is a quiet island of permanence amidst the change and uncertainty of the modern world.

Crevices and Caves:
The Excitement of the Scarp Edge
Nottawasaga Bluffs and Singhampton Caves
Nottawasaga Bluffs

Trail Length: **5.6 kilometres**

Time: **3 hours (with time to explore)**

Grade: **Moderate, except for the more strenuous climb into the caves**

Access: **From Singhampton, take Concession 11 and the bridge over the Mad River; then turn left (east) on 17-18 Sideroad, right (south) on Concession 10, and left (east) on 15-16 Sideroad.**

Map: ***Guide to the Bruce Trail:* map 22: Devil's Glen**

Parking: **There is a gravel parking lot on the south side of 15-16 Sideroad, directly opposite the last farm.**

About 20 kilometres south of Collingwood near the town of Singhampton, there are some exciting hiking possibilities. Two of our favourites are Nottawasaga Bluffs and the Singhampton Caves. Both give you an opportunity to climb literally into the bowels of the escarpment, into a world of cool green mosses and ferns and the black silence of the underworld.

Nottawasaga Bluffs is a small little-known conservation area of rolling farmland, upland forest and limestone crags. Located about 6 kilometres southeast of Singhampton, it is a fascinating area, especially for those who wish to explore the network of crevices and caves that dot its southern bluff. Obviously, however, there is an element of danger; never explore the caves alone, and equip yourself with proper footgear and a flashlight.

From the parking area on the south side of 15-16 Sideroad, opposite the last farm, head south on the blue-blazed cart track for .6 kilometres. On the way, you pass a 1991 reforestation project of the Boy Scouts. In the fields, which are lying fallow, is a profusion of summer wildflowers.

As you approach the bluff, the ground rises slightly. Just before a clearing, the cart track intersects the Bruce Trail. Turn right through a young maple bush; to the left is an abandoned field now being reforested. You soon reach a small wilderness camping area with a picnic table and privy. It is a tranquil spot and, except for the lack of water, would make an excellent place to get away from it all. (Those who do camp here can descend the scarp via the main trail to a small stream at its base. The obvious presence of beavers, however, should remind you that drinking water has to be filtered or boiled for at least fifteen minutes.)

At the camping area is a sign directing you to the Keyhole Trail. Only .5 kilometres in length, it is a dramatic short hike. It quickly descends into a crevice, and the temperature plunges. Ferns and mosses cover the walls as the crevice narrows to shoulder width. Watch for the blue blazes, as there are other unmarked crevices that invite exploration. Finally the trail leads down to the Keyhole. Here you have to take off your pack, set it on the other side and then pop your body through the opening in the rock wall. The *Bruce Trail Guidebook* calls this path, "a fascinating route for the adventuresome." (If it is too difficult, however, you can cross over the outcrop before descending into the final crevice.)

After climbing through the Keyhole, turn right and follow the trail as it drops below the escarpment edge. It wanders among cedars before reaching the white blazes of the main trail.

Now turn left. It is a good climb on an old cart track to return to the top of the escarpment. Continue to the right on the white-blazed main trail. (The blue blazes lead directly to the campsite.) The trail wanders through a birch, maple and balsam fir woods and then along the precipitous edge of the escarpment. From the lookouts, you peer down on the talus slopes below and the farms and green fields to the south. In the fall, the coloured leaves can make it a spectacular vista.

At the end of these lookouts are the Best Caves, named after a previous landowner. The name, however, is appropriate, for it is believed that some thirty to forty caves honeycomb this area. The largest is the Well, a deep cave that is more enticing than many of the commercially available caves on the escarpment. Its entrance is marked by faint red and yellow paint blazes. It is ten metres deep and has four levels, the deepest of which is covered in ice even in the height of summer. Almost two decades ago in late August, one of the authors' young son, though edu-

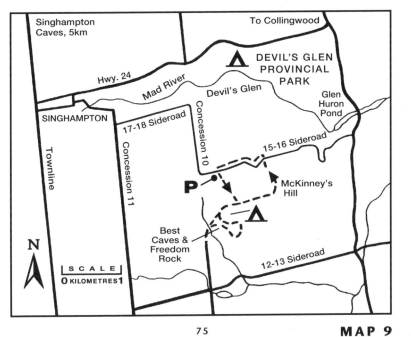

MAP 9

9

Nottawasaga Bluffs & Singhampton Caves

Enormous elm logs are measured in this sawmill scene taken in 1907.
– Credit: Ontario Ministry of Agriculture and Food, R.R. Sallows Collection, H of A 536

cated about the Trail User's Code, was so enthralled that he broke off an icicle about fifteen centimetres long. On that hot summer's day it became his "Nottawasaga Bluffs popsicle."

The caves can provide hours of fascinating exploration, but remember the need for boots and a flashlight.

Next, continue on the main trail for about 100 metres and then follow the yellow blazes on the right for a short distance to Freedom Rock. This side trail may not have been maintained recently but it reveals an unexpected glimpse into the past.

Freedom Rock is an outcropping broken off from the escarpment. The formation is similar to the standing rock at the commercially developed Scenic Caves in the Blue Mountains above Collingwood. But what is so surprising at Freedom Rock is the collection of aphorisms that have been lovingly inscribed in the rock. In the tradition of nineteenth-century liberals, many concern some aspect of freedom: access to the courts, the right to free education, and the need for land rationing. Conservative in expression, they reflect a love of the land and a concern for the "little man." Examples include: To Be Fully Free One Must Farm, The Trend Toward Estate Farming is Ruining The Rural Way of Life, Individuals Are Diamonds.

None is the careless graffiti of our age; each has been carefully chiselled into the stone. Both script and theme tells something about the attitudes of past; a testament to the "Anglo-Saxon Protestant way of life" reflects the religious conflicts that were once a factor in rural Ontario, and the anti-immigration "Canada for the Canadains [sic]: China for Chinese," reminds us that racial prejudice has been around for a long time.

Over the twenty years that we have been aware of Freedom Rock, the inscriptions have weathered a great deal. Some are now almost illegible and will soon fade into the rock, erasing forever the thoughts of their maker or makers. One is left to ponder their origins. Who would have cared enough to do this much work?

At the bottom of the scarp, marked by a yellow blaze, is a cave called the Tomb—just large enough to hold one body. It too must contain a story. Is this where a rock-carver received inspiration?

Next, return to the top of the escarpment and follow the white blazes as they swing through a young maple woods interspersed with birch. The trail takes you past the campsite, and after .8 kilometres, you reach the blue trail that will take you back to the parking lot.

If you have time, continue straight ahead on the main trail for the other loop of the figure-eight circuit. The well-defined path leads to a stile and an abandoned farm field. In the summer you will be walking through wildflowers that are waist high. Next comes a pleasant woods where the trail swings north (or left) on a ridge with cultivated fields below you to the east. After 1.5 kilometres you reach the 15-16 Sideroad, now a seldom-used single track, which leads you in a westerly direction (left) back to the parking area.

Singhampton Caves

Trail Length:	**2 kilometres**
Time:	**2 hours (with time to explore)**
Grade:	**Strenuous**
Access:	**From Singhampton, continue north on the Townline for 6 kilometres.**
Map:	***Guide to the Bruce Trail:* map 23: Pretty River**
Parking:	**Where the Townline dead-ends (and a gravel road turns sharply to the left), park on the east side of the road.**

The crevices of the Keyhole Trail are the result of the fracturing of the limestone along the fault lines of the escarpment edge. This process can result in caves such as are found to the south at Mount Nemo. The most accessible and perhaps the most beautiful caves along the escarpment are those north of Singhampton.

From the parking place at the end of the Townline, follow the white blazes north for 330 metres through a forest of young maples and small pines to the escarpment edge. Instead of turning right on the main trail, continue straight to the lookout, but heed the Cliff Area: Danger sign. Ahead of you lies the green forest canopy of the Pretty River Valley. On the far side, you can see the straight line of the Townline where it continues north again.

Now take the blue-blazed trail to the right into the crevice, but be careful. The cool air creates condensation on the limestone, making for slippery footing. Descend by a sturdy ladder into the green world of mosses and ferns that cloak the walls of the cave. Continue through the crevice and follow the blue blazes as the route scrambles back up the scarp edge. It is a strenuous but spectacular short trail, and with proper care, should pose no problem for the fit hiker.

You are now back on the white-blazed main trail. It takes you east along the scarp brow, then descends through a cut in the cliff and drops steeply to the base of the escarpment. After about .7 kilometres you will come to a yellow-blazed trail on the left. (Remember that a yellow blaze is a side trail off a side trail, frequently a connecting route.) This recently constructed route, known as the Standing Rock Side Trail, is a spectacular addition for anyone interested in the geology of the escarpment.

As it has not yet been discovered by a lot of hikers, the treadway can sometimes be obscured. Look for the birch logs that have been used to line parts of the trail.

The path leads across the base of the scarp through a young forest to a great rock pillar that stands 80 metres north of the escarpment edge. From its top, hangs a rusty steel cable, leftover, perhaps from logging days when timber was winched down the slope. The trail turns sharply up the jumbled rock debris of the talus slope, making for some rough scrambling. Suddenly, however, it pops out through a tight crevice into the Singhampton Cave, just at the base of the ladder you had previously descended. From here, it is a short walk back to your car.

The Standing Rock Side Trail is a dramatic conclusion to your day's hiking and a journey literally into the depths of time—430 million years of it.

A good camping base for your explorations of the area is Devil's Glen Provincial Park, just a short distance along Highway 24 east of Singhampton. It is a small quiet park perched on the escarpment edge. Noted for spectacular Blue Mountains scenery and an excellent view of the surrounding countryside, it is a convenient stopover while on holiday in the Huronia area and a good place to relax for a few days. For those who don't want to camp yet would like to prolong their visit, the Collingwood area has a wide variety of accommodation.

North of Singhampton, at a point on the Singhampton Moraine overlooking Edward Lake, you can visit the highest elevation in Southern Ontario, some 546 metres above sea level. And if you want some gentler walking or a bike ride along the base of the escarpment, try the 32-kilometre Georgian Trail, a multi-use trail that follows the old CN rail bed between Collingwood and Meaford.

Finally, if you think you deserve a special treat, try Chez Michel, a very popular French restaurant on Highway 26 just west of Mountain Road. (The Georgian Trail passes just behind the restaurant.) It is one of those memorable places that combine a relaxed atmosphere with an ample wine list and great food, and it's a perfect place to end a hard day on the trail.

History and High Points
The Petun Loop and Pretty River Valley
The Petun Loop

Trail Length: **5.5 kilometres**

Time: **2.5 hours**

Grade: **A strenuous climb up the escarpment; otherwise moderate**

Access: **From Highway 26 at the west end of Collingwood, turn left just before the tourist information building onto Mountain Road. Drive to Grey County Road 19. Turn left (south) onto Grey 19, which runs south for 3 kilometres, then turns west. Follow it up the escarpment for 3 kilometres to the 2nd Line.**

Map: **Guide to the Bruce Trail: map 23: Pretty River**

Parking: **On the south side of Grey County Road 19 at the 2nd Line. (Look for the white blazes of the Bruce Trail.)**

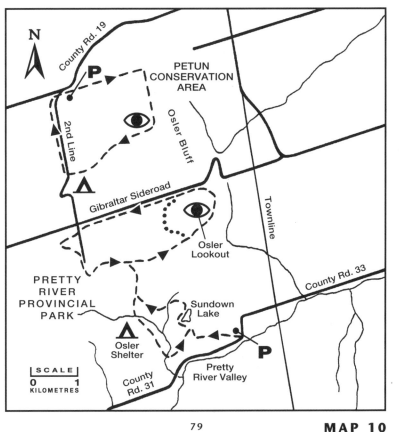

MAP 10

10

Petun Loop & Pretty River Valley

The Blue Mountains section of the Bruce Trail offers some very attractive loop hikes. The closest one to Collingwood is the Petun Loop, interesting both for its history and for its vistas across Georgian Bay. For centuries, people have been drawn to its mountain slopes. An Indian tribe, nineteenth-century millionaires, and twentieth-century vacationers have all in their turn fallen captive to its potent charm.

About 350 years ago, the Petun or Tionontati Indians lived in a series of villages along the slopes of the escarpment. They grew crops of corn, squash, pumpkins and beans and lived communally in longhouses. Then, in November 1649, most of the tribe was massacred by invading Seneca. The few survivors fled to the west; their descendants are found today in the United States.

Just to the north of the hiking loop is the former location of a large Petun village; records of early explorers and archaeological evidence confirm the site. The Petun chose it because they thought it was easily defended and had an abundance of wood, water and good soil. But after the slaughter, two hundred years were to elapse before settlement returned to the area.

Osler Bluff, rising abruptly more than 200 metres from the farmland at its base, dominates the escarpment sweep through the Blue Mountains southeast of Collingwood. The magnificent view prompted Britton Bath Osler, a prominent Victorian lawyer, to construct a palatial summer residence in the last decade of the nineteenth century. He called it *Kionontio*, Petun Indian for top of the hill, and indeed the vista from the bluff is the highlight of today's Petun Loop Trail.

From Grey County Road 19, hike east on the blue-blazed side trail. After a short distance, the road deteriorates to a cart track, and the route may be muddy and show the scars of mountain bikes, but it provides a pleasant walk with fine views over the bay.

Above a large farm pond, the trail turns right (south); look for the Bruce Trail diamond. As you begin to climb the escarpment, you are entering the property of the Osler Bluff Ski Club. Please respect their generosity in allowing hikers access to their land by observing the Trail Users' Code and by remaining on the defined route. Initially, the trail passes through scrub vegetation that is reclaiming abandoned farm land; then it enters mixed forest. As it passes the reservoir of the ski club, the route becomes steep and irregular. You scramble past centuries-old limestone boulders that have tumbled from the scarp. A good pair of hiking boots and a walking stick will make this section easier.

You then begin to climb directly up the escarpment via a steep, narrow crevice, perhaps the steepest incline along the entire Bruce Trail. There is a hand cable to give you support, but remember that you are responsible for your own safety.

When you get to the top of Osler Bluff, there are commanding views over Collingwood and the southern end of Georgian Bay. Directly ahead of you are a lighthouse and a grain elevator, eloquent reminders of Collingwood's heyday as a prosperous Great Lakes port. To your right,

Silver Creek nears the edge of the Niagara Escarpment.
– Richard Armstrong

*Looking over the treetops towards Orangeville,
from a high point in Mono Cliffs Provincial Park.*
– Richard Armstrong

Winter at Inglis Falls
– Richard Armstrong

*The glowing colours of autumn reflected in
the deep, still waters of Crawford Lake.*
– Lorne Geddes

The sea stacks on Flowerpot Island
– Lorne Geddes

Autumn splendour at
Silver Creek Conservation Area
– Lorne Geddes

Sunset at Cyprus Lake
– Lorne Geddes

A lone spruce stands guard above Georgian Bay.
– Richard Armstrong

the bay sweeps round to the white sands of Wasaga, and in the distance are Hope, Beckwith and Christian islands. This is a perfect place to stop for lunch and to reflect on the beauties of the land.

The blue-blazed trail then continues south through a mixed hardwood forest. Soon you meet the white blazes of the main Bruce Trail; follow them to the right (west) into the open fields of the Petun Conservation Area. This conservation authority property of mixed forest, scrubland and grassy meadows is as yet undeveloped. You may notice that the edges of the abandoned fields are lined with large boulders; these are erratics, fragments of rock that were pried free from their bedrock by glaciers and carried along for hundreds of kilometres before being abandoned. Their tidy placement along fence lines bears silent witness to the toils of the nineteenth-century pioneer farmers.

On the property is a rough camping area for backpackers. It boasts the world's biggest picnic table, its size (we can only assume) a deterrent to thieves! A trail to the right leads down the scarp for 50 metres to a perpetually flowing spring; the water is clear and cool, but again, remember to treat it before drinking.

The trail continues west along a fence line before descending for 450 metres via a stream bed filled with ferns and tumbled limestone boulders. Just before you get to the road, seepage from the escarpment can make for wet footing, so take care. On the road, turn right and the white blazes will lead you 1.2 kilometres back to your car.

On your descent of this seldom-travelled road, you will notice Castle Glen Estates with its modern ski chalets. Behind them, however, lies a ruin of a far more romantic age. The Osler Castle is inaccessible to the hiker, but from this vantage point, you can see the fieldstone granite walls, all that remain of one man's extravagant dream.

Bruce Trail Association past-president and historian, Alan Stacey, has researched the story. Osler was a prominent Ontario lawyer who, among other assignments, had been a prosecuting attorney at the trial of Louis Riel. Osler's wife, Carrie, was crippled by arthritis, and Osler felt that a summer home might improve her condition. Therefore, in 1893 he purchased 815 hectares at the top of the escarpment and began the construction of Kionontio.

An anonymous chronicler wrote that "Nothing was spared to make it imposing. That was the way successful men in the last century showed their wealth." Local fieldstone boulders were used to face the exterior walls of the fifteen-room summer home, resplendent with turreted chimneys. An arched stone doorway, covered veranda and large airy bay windows graced the front facade. Heavy furnishings came largely from England, a fact only too well known to the sweating teamsters who had to haul them up the Mountain Road to the isolated mansion. Water from Silver Creek was force-pumped up the escarpment and then gravity-fed into the house.

The landscaping included terraced lawns, rose and peony beds, and wrought-iron gates emblazoned with the name Kionontio. Later, stocked

trout ponds were added, and Osler even toyed with the idea of enclosing some of the wild deer within a fenced park.

By the autumn of 1894, the estate was complete and Osler chartered a Grand Trunk parlour car for guests up to Collingwood. Hopes were high that Carrie's health might improve. Her mother-in-law wrote to her, "My heart has been with you and sorry I am to know that you have been so poorly lately. After a while you may be able to drive out and enjoy the fresh air, hear the robins chirp their spring notes and from your window you can see or smell the green buds showing new life and the promise of summer." Sadly, however, Carrie never lived to see a summer at Kionontio; she died in May of the next year.

Never did Osler Castle realize its potential. In 1901, Osler himself died,

An enigmatic group poses for an unknown photographer amidst the tumbled limestone and fallen trees at the base of the escarpment in the Blue Mountains, circa 1885.
– Credit: Collingwood Museum

and Kionontio's story came to an end. Virtually abandoned, the furnishings, structure and property succumbed to the ravages of vandalism and time, and were seized for back taxes. Perhaps Andrew Armitage, in *The Day the Governor-General Came to Town,* best described the romantic spell that the ruins still evoke: "Kionontio—the top of the hill—the Osler Castle that for a few brief summers was a place of enchantment—and then no more."

The Pretty River Valley

Trail Length: **5.4 kilometres or 13 kilometres**

Time: **2.5 hours or 6 hours**

Grade: **Moderate, except for a steady climb up the escarpment on the longer of the two loops**

Access: **From Highway 24, turn west on Simcoe 33, at a point 5 kilometres south of Collingwood (or 6 kilometres north of Duntroon). After about 7 kilometres, Simcoe 33 crosses the Townline and becomes Grey 31. After 500 metres, it swings left and then right beside the Pretty River.**

Map: **Guide to the Bruce Trail: map 23: Pretty River** *(see map on page 79)*

Parking: **On the right side of Grey 31, where it meets the river, there is a small parking area. If it is full, there is a larger gravel parking lot 400 metres back on the south side of the road.**

Another favourite hiking area is the Pretty River Valley. Much of the land is owned by the Ministry of Natural Resources; although it has not yet been developed, it is one of ten parks that the Niagara Escarpment Plan has defined as locations for public information and education. In the past, the area has been plagued by four-wheel-drive all-terrain vehicles and by mountain bikes, both of which have done considerable damage to the trails. But despite these problems, it is still one of our favourite hiking spots, especially with the coloured leaves of fall. We remember especially one spectacular late-October day over a decade ago. It had snowed the previous night on the top of the escarpment. The coloured leaves had set the valley slopes ablaze, and the sky and Georgian Bay were intensely blue in the brilliant sunshine.

In the 1840s, a Scottish settlement opened the valley. Your drive along Grey 19 will have taken you past the graveyard of the West Nottawasaga Presbyterian Church. Some of those pioneers are buried there beneath tombstones that record 150 years of history. The landscape, too, has a Scottish quality about it, with its rolling fields and century-old farmhouses where the names on the mailboxes still have a Scottish ring. Some (such as Currie) recur frequently.

From the parking area, follow the white blazes of the Bruce Trail over a small stile. The trail follows a farm field for a short distance before beginning its climb up the valley slopes. After a kilometre you reach a trail intersection; turn right and follow the blue blazes to Sundown Lake.

The trail climbs up and over a ridge to reach this hidden kettle lake. It is a gem of a place, a relic of glacial times when a block of ice detached itself from the retreating mass to create the depression in which the lake formed. The frogs croak to announce your arrival, and on a sandy point by the water is a dock and a picnic bench. Here the troubles of the twentieth-century world seem far away!

The path continues along the side of the lake and over rolling hillocks through a mixed forest, then climbs a wooded ridge to meet the main

Petun Loop & Pretty River Valley

trail. Here you have a choice; you can turn left to complete a 5.4-kilometre hike to return to your car, or you can turn right for a full day's hike of 13 kilometres.

If you opt for the long hike, the trail climbs steadily. Stay on the main trail, which takes you to the north rim of the valley. At the top, the white blazes lead sharply left through a pine plantation and a maple woods to the Gibraltar Sideroad.

Instead, take the blue-blazed trail, which leads straight ahead to the Osler Lookout. From this vantage point, you have a splendid view of the green farm fields below, the wooded slopes of the far side of the valley, the Collingwood elevator, and the sandy crescent of Wasaga Beach.

At the lookout, the blazes end; however, an unmarked but frequently used trail continues to the north and brings you out onto the Gibraltar Sideroad. If there are no signs, continue on this route, but if there are No Trespassing signs or red circles on the trees, you will have to return to the main trail and follow it north; it too brings you to the Gibraltar Sideroad. The unmarked path along the escarpment edge lined by dramatic crevices is the much more interesting route.

At the Gibraltar Sideroad, turn left. It is a seldom-used pleasant country lane, shaded by trees and with farm fields on either side. After about .5 kilometres the white blazes of the main trail intersect the sideroad, but continue straight ahead as far as the intersection with the 2nd Line and then turn left on the cart track to the northern entrance to the Pretty River Valley. Here the state of the ground tells you that the sign, Closed To Motorized Vehicles, has proven ineffective.

Instead of following their scarred route, follow the blue blazes to the left to the highest point on the entire Bruce Trail. There is no longer a sign; all that remains to mark the spot is a broken metal pole on the left. Step over the fence and head out into the abandoned field. Under the tree in the shade is a good picnic spot, but remember to leave no trace of your visit.

After .5 kilometres, this blue trail rejoins the main trail; turn right to descend into the valley. Follow the white blazes downhill and across a stream on an old logging bridge. Here you will find a cleared area for camping, and 100 metres up a badly rutted track on the right is the Osler Shelter, one of the few remaining shelters built in the 1970s when the vision for the Bruce Trail held the promise of a backpacking route from Niagara to Tobermory. Unfortunately, a combination of government underfunding and vandalism has prevented the realization of this dream.

The main trail then passes through the second-growth forest that now covers the valley floor. It is easy pleasant hiking along the banks of the bubbling stream and past old ruins and apple trees. Soon the trail climbs to the junction with the Sundown Lake trail. From here, you retrace your steps via the white blazes for 1 kilometre to where you parked your car.

One of the fascinations of the Pretty River Valley is its multitude of hiking possibilities. You can limit yourself to a short venture such as a two-hour 5.4-kilometre circuit of Sundown Lake, or by combining the Valley with the Petun loop to the north, make a taxing 20-kilometre circuit that will take a full day. Whichever alternative you choose, the beauty and variety of the valley will draw you back.

An Undiscovered Hiking Treasure
The Kolapore Uplands Wilderness

Trail Length: **8.4 kilometres. (The trail network totals 60 kilometres.)**

Time: **3 hours**

Grade: **Moderate**

Access: **From Highway 10, turn east at Flesherton on Highway 4. After about 12 kilometres, turn north on Grey County Road 2. Travel 14 kilometres to Kolapore.**
From Highway 26 about 2 kilometres east of Thornbury, turn south on Grey County Road 2. Travel 15 kilometres to Kolapore.

Map: **Because of the complexity of the trail network, purchase a trail map from the Ravenna General Store, 4.7 kilometres north of the parking area, or from Kolapore Uplands Ski Trails, Box 6647, Station A, Toronto, Ontario M5W 1X4.**

Parking: **A gravel parking area is located on the east side of Grey County Road 2, some 400 metres north of the Kolapore Church. The trail network begins to the west of the road, just at the southern end of the curve.**

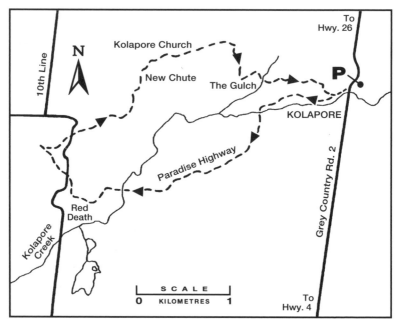

Kolapore Uplands

11 **MAP 11**   86

In the uplands between the Blue Mountains and the Beaver Valley, there is a rugged semiwilderness area that contains 60 kilometres of marked trails. This network has been developed and is maintained by the University of Toronto Outing Club, primarily for cross-country skiers. But it also makes a fine hiking resource; there are enough options to keep you returning for many a day's exploration.

The first white settlers arrived in the area in the mid-nineteenth century. The original Kolapore settlement was called Paradise, but when a post office was opened, it was discovered that there was already a town by that name. The new name of Kolapore was adopted to commemorate a recent battle in India. In the 1860s and 1870s, the forests attracted lumberjacks who, by the early 1900s, had decimated the timber resources. But during this brief period, Kolapore was a bustling community of three mills; the ruins of one can still be seen on the east side of the road. Despite the fact that the soils were thin and poor in quality, settlers attempted to farm much of the cleared land. Today, the foundations of ruined farmhouses and barns scattered throughout the area are silent evidence of the failure of many of these ventures. Much of the abandoned pasture land is now reverting to forest.

Most of the trail system is located on land now owned by government agencies. The Ministry of Natural Resources, for example, has purchased twelve thousand hectares for the Kolapore Uplands Resource Management Area. Other parcels belong to the Grey-Sauble Conservation Authority and Grey County. As well, several sections of the trail cross private land whose owners have generously permitted the outing club to use their land. Therefore, it is especially important to observe the Trail Users' Code, staying on the marked trails and not littering or building a fire.

With such a complex network, you must carry a trail map; otherwise it is easy to become confused. The map is printed on a scale of 1:20,000 with contour intervals of 25 feet (7.6 metres), and it describes all routes. Proceeds from the map sales are used for the maintenance and development of the trail system, so remember that when you buy your map your money is supporting a good cause.

To avoid getting lost, it is also important that you understand the signage system. Trails are marked with orange triangular blazes. At many of the intersections, signs indicate the distance to various destinations. As well, at each intersection, a large yellow triangular sign points to the number of the next intersection in that direction. Together with the map, these signs let you know where you are.

An attractive 8.4-kilometre loop starting at the parking area is created by the Paradise Highway, New Chute and Kolapore Church trails. On the west side of the road at the south end of the curve, you will find an old logging track that takes you into the cedar bush just north of the wetlands.

Soon you reach junction 18. Take the clearly signed Paradise Highway as it follows a shelf above the river. The trail passes over rolling terrain, through mature hardwood forest, pine plantation and abandoned farm fields. Old fence lines and the remains of farm implements are reminders

Kolapore Uplands

11

of a bygone era; today, only the pleasant sounds of the rushing stream remain.

The bridges along the route are well built. After about 3 kilometres when the trail recrosses Kolapore Creek and a marsh area, you will notice a strange-looking structure. Its purpose is to control the water level. Designed by the Ministry of Natural Resources and known as a beaver baffler, it is supposed to keep the water flowing through the beaver dam and thus avoid the flooding out of the trail. It has not, however, been an unqualified success. In some places the beavers have simply surrounded the intake pipe with a dam. Clearly, much more ingenuity is needed if we are going to succeed in our attempts to outsmart these industrious engineers!

Just past the marshy area at intersection 54, swing left past the old apple trees, another reminder of pioneer farm days. The path soon climbs steeply up to Red Death Lookout. It is a fine spot for a lunch break, with its pleasant views to the south.

Dropping off this outlier (an outcropping of rock separated from the main escarpment), the trail then crosses the little-used 10th Concession road into a young maple-beech forest. It swings to the right from intersections 26 to 27 to 59 and again crosses the road. It next follows the flat track in an easterly direction to intersection 24, where it rejoins the Paradise Highway, running north. At the next junction, turn right at the old maple tree and climb the expert ski trail called New Chute. (In winter, this is a very challenging run with several moguls.) Soon you join the Kolapore Church Trail at intersection 21 as it heads east across gently rolling terrain through a mature hardwood forest. For variety, at intersection 56, turn right and descend the steep slopes of the Gulch, another expert ski run across the headwaters of Kolapore Creek. Soon you rejoin the Kolapore Church trail for an easy walk back to the car park.

These trails also provide the best wilderness cross-country skiing in Southern Ontario. Once you have hiked them, you will want to return in the winter. Names such as Red Death Hill should give some inkling of what you are likely to find. It is very important to remember that most of the trails were designed primarily for intermediate and advanced skiers. Only one section of the trail network (the County Forest) is suitable for novices. Several of the hills are extremely difficult; you should be an experienced skier and carry the basic equipment listed on the trail map. Also, although the trails are carefully marked and cleared, they are not groomed, and following a snowstorm, you may have to break trail. Remember that you use the trails at your own risk.

But when the rest of Southern Ontario is wet and grey, Kolapore often has good skiing; during a normal winter, the ski season extends from late December to mid-March. In some seasons, it can extend for another month in either direction. Frequently in the spring, the woods offer good skiing long after most of the snow has disappeared from the neighbouring fields.

This whole network of trails is an outstanding example of what can be accomplished by volunteers; both skiing and hiking opportunities are a result of the efforts of members of the University of Toronto Outing Club. The public can use the trails at no charge, but only because club volunteers devote over a thousand hours annually to constructing trails, building bridges, clearing deadfall and new growth, and erecting signs. Donations towards trail-maintenance costs are greatly appreciated.

For supplies, the nearest general store (with gas pumps) is in Ravenna, 4.7 kilometres north of the parking lot on Grey Country Road 2. Bed and breakfast accommodation is also available here. Throughout the Thornbury-Clarksburg area are a number of charming B & Bs. Especially in the winter, booking ahead is essential.

About 10 kilometres south of Kolapore there is another hiking treasure known only to a few. From Grey County Road 2, signs clearly indicate the Madelaine Graydon Conservation Area on the west side of the road, south of the turnoff to Feversham. It is a beautiful area, rich in geological and biological interest.

The Feversham Gorge begins on private property at an old mill dam and extends downstream along the Beaver River. Its vertical limestone walls tower 24 metres over the crystal-clear river and are cloaked with conifers and ferns. The river is spring-fed and a natural haven for brook trout. Here it is relatively shallow with several inviting pools and bubbling rapids.

Although somewhat hard to reach, the cliffs are a botanist's paradise, home to a number of rare ferns, mosses and liverworts. These plants thrive in the permanent shade created by the trees and limestone cliffs. At the top of the gorge, you will find a 1.5-kilometre hiking trail. Walk from the south end of the parking lot in a clockwise direction through the mixed coniferous and deciduous forest. Lookouts and a stairway add to the enjoyment of this scenic, if somewhat strenuous, short trail.

The beauties of both Kolapore and Feversham will tempt you back often. And one of the joys will be the absence of people; frequently, you will have the paths to yourself. They are treasures that deserve to be discovered by more people, but, we hope, never by too many at once!

Chasms and Clefts, Cliffs and Cascades
The Trails of the Beaver Valley Uplands

High on the eastern shoulder of the Beaver Valley there is an upland area cut through by many creeks and streams. At first glance, it seems wild and remote, and indeed, settlement here has always been sparse. The isolated farmsteads that dot the landscape tell the visitor that only a very few settlers chose to try to wrest a living from shallow, stony soils that proved so unreceptive to cultivation. And certainly no settlements of any size grew up. A few tiny hamlets did develop, some around mills located on local creeks, others at crossroads.

But an area that was so inhospitable to the nineteenth-century settler is a delight to the twentieth-century hiker.

From its elevated shelf, the land commands sweeping vistas over both the Beaver Valley and Nottawasaga Bay. Time and again, you will turn a

corner and halt in your tracks, overwhelmed by the panorama unfolding before you. In places where the trail takes you along the escarpment rim, you will find the edge cleft by deep crevices. Sometimes you emerge on the top of a sheer cliff to a breathtaking view across a beautiful valley, where forested slopes give way to meadowland at the bottom. Throughout the area, much of the old farmland is returning to a wild state, but now and then you will come across a working farm where an old farmstead, with its little pond, barn, surrounding cattle pastures and cultivated fields, presents a picture of perfect rural harmony.

And it is a harmony that few people disturb. On each of the three loops described here, you can often walk without meeting anyone, even on holiday weekends. The hikes, ranging in length from 9.2 to 3.5 kilometres, take you through some magnificent countryside, and each offers it own distinct treasures, waiting to be discovered.

A family affair. All the Mitchells, both men and women, lend a hand threshing the sweet clover crop in an upland meadow at Redwing in 1914.
– Credit: Township of Collingwood Archives

Beaver Valley Uplands

12

Trail Length: **9.2 kilometres**

Time: **4–5 hours**

Grade: **Moderate to strenuous**

Access: **From Grey County Road 13 about 4.5 kilometres north of Eugenia, turn right along 1 Sideroad, signposted Duncan. The road goes east, then turns north. Just past Duncan Lake the road turns east again. You are now on 9-10 Sideroad, and after 2.75 kilometres, you will see Duncan Crevice Caves Provincial Park on your right.**
If you are approaching from the north, about 5 kilometres south of Heathcote, where County Road 13 jogs west, continue straight ahead on the Townline for 4 kilometres to the Duncan crossroads. Turn left onto 9-10 Sideroad.

Map: ***Guide to the Bruce Trail:* map 25: Kolapore**

Parking: **At Duncan Crevice Caves Provincial Park**

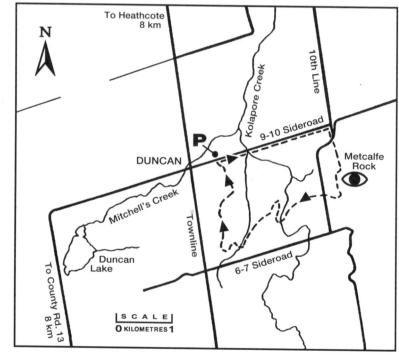

Beaver Valley Uplands

For the first 2.5 kilometres, you follow the unblazed 9-10 Sideroad east. If it looks endless, stretching out in front of you, take heart; it is a very pretty walk and you rarely meet any vehicular traffic. In summer the route is made particularly pleasing by the profusion of colourful wild-flowers along the shoulders. As you walk along, the nodding heads of blue flax, daisy, Jacob's ladder and Queen Anne's lace all compete for your attention.

After a descent to cross Mill Creek, keep a sharp lookout to the left as you climb up again. Near the top of the rise, you suddenly get a view of the shoreline and blue water of Nottawasaga Bay.

At a T-junction, turn right on the 10th Line and follow it for about 100 metres. When the road veers around to the right, continue straight ahead along a track leading into the trees. The blue blazes of the Duncan Side Trail begin here. You will find yourself passing through a lightly wooded area with open country to your left. After about .7 kilometres, the white-blazed Bruce Trail comes in from the left, and you continue south, now following white blazes.

The path makes a slight descent into a more heavily wooded area. The increasingly rocky terrain and thick growth of old cedars signal that you are nearing the edge of the escarpment. A track to your right takes you a few metres to the first of several superb lookouts over Kolapore Creek Valley. You are standing on the top of Metcalfe Rock, and there is a sheer drop under your feet to the talus slopes and the valley floor. In some places, large pieces of rock have fractured and broken away from the cliff, leaving yawning gaps. Cedars, twisted by the brutal elements into curious shapes, cling tenaciously to the top of the rock and, impossibly, to the sheer rock face.

Apart from being stunted and a bit crooked, the cedars don't look all that special, and until recently they were thought to be part of the second-growth tree cover along the escarpment that followed the nine-teenth-century logging boom. But when Dr. Doug Larsen, professor of botany at the University of Guelph, started to examine them, he found that rather than being sixty, eighty, or even one hundred years old, they are five hundred, seven hundred and, in some cases, even one thousand years old. The discovery of similar specimens along the length of the escarpment suggests that the thin line of trees that cling to the rocks is in fact a complete but very small ecosystem and, quite likely, according to Dr. Larsen, "the oldest, most intact and most undisturbed place in eastern North America." The trees have survived because of their inaccessibility; until recently, humans have not been able to blunder in and destroy them. The fact that we can now get to them puts them in danger, for Dr. Larsen has discovered that even slight trampling causes the fragile balance of the ecosystem to change. Now that we known how precious these trees are, we must not forget that each one of us bears part of the awesome responsibility of ensuring that they are protected.

When you can take your eyes off the cedars, look at the splendid view across the tranquil valley to the opposite rim. Sometimes, when the weather has closed in, mist boils up from the bottom of the valley, veiling the landscape and adding a touch of drama and mystery.

Continuing along the trail, you pass by more crevices along the edge. Then the path makes a sharp right turn, leading you down over large rocks into a spectacular narrow gorge, some 30 metres high, formed when huge slabs of limestone tilted and slumped away from the escarpment face.

No matter what time of year you are there and whatever the weather, the gorge is a magical place. Suddenly you find yourself in a cool chamber with a rock-strewn floor and perpendicular walls. Lichens, mosses and ferns cover the walls and the fallen rocks with a multi-textured green mantle. In early summer, exquisite flowers such as miniature aquilegia and delicate mitrewort embroider the green face of the rock with tiny points of colour. High above your head, large trees that seem to sprout from the rock face thrust upwards, straining towards the light and sun.

The sense of magic is even greater perhaps in the rain, for then the whole place seems to be shedding copious tears as you stand watching the rivulets run down the rock face, hearing nothing but the gentle sound of dripping water and suddenly feeling the urge to speak only in a whisper.

The passage through the gorge is short but quite strenuous and requires care. Essentially you descend through three chambers, each separated from the next by a steep, narrow rock barrier. There are plenty of good footholds and handholds, but the rocks are covered in vegetation and, therefore, slippery at all times. When it's wet, you need to be extra careful. As you scramble through the three chambers, holes in the rock face tell you that caves are present. If you put your hand or face near one of the openings, you will feel a rush of cold air, even on the warmest day. This is a popular place for spelunkers, but if you feel tempted to try it, remember that caving is a potentially hazardous sport; you must be properly equipped and know what you are doing.

The gorge discharges you at the foot of a high cliff, and you get a good look at the jumbled talus at the bottom as you follow the blazes for about 100 metres through woods to cross a stream. On the other side, you suddenly find yourself in a sunlit meadow. The change of mood is astonishing as you make your way through a riotous display of colour fashioned by purple spotted knapweed, white daisies and Queen Anne's lace and yellow ranunculus.

The trail leads you across 10th Line and over a stile into a field. Walk along the perimeter of a couple of fields, turning right, then left and eventually over a stile to head into woods, where the path gradually swings south. Soon you will hear the sound of water below as the trail passes along a shelf above the river. It follows Kolapore Creek for about .5 kilometres before descending to a wooden bridge and doubling back on the other side. You start to climb again, at first gently, then more steeply, all the time passing through graceful tall hardwoods that form a high overhead canopy. Higher up, the terrain becomes more rocky, and just before you reach the top of the slope, you traverse a patch of loose scree, but there is a well-marked path, so it is not difficult.

At the top, the trail swings around to the south and brings you out into a flat open area on top of the west rim of the valley. This is past the halfway point and a great place for lunch. From your rocky perch, you get wonderful views over the valley to Metcalfe Rock and the eastern rim.

Now the trail takes you south on a gentle descent. Open country gives way to trees; then you follow the perimeter of a couple of farm fields before reentering woods and crossing a stream. You begin to climb once more through a mature hardwood forest until you arrive at Pinnacle Rock, a large outcrop.

There is a short, steep and fairly strenuous scramble up a rock-strewn slope to get to the top of the escarpment. (The rocks are heavily moss-covered, so it's tricky at any time, but in wet weather you must be very careful.) At the top, the white blazes veer left, but you turn right to follow the blue-blazed Duncan Side Trail.

You are now walking north along a heavily wooded ridge. Here and there, if you approach the edge, you will get good views east again across Kolapore Creek Valley, and, at one point, there is a sudden long vista over to Nottaswasaga Bay. Many crevices line your route. Deep fissures lie very close to the path, and you cross over one of them on a rock bridge. Anyone with children should be particularly careful, as one slip could spell disaster.

After about a kilometre, you come out into open country, and, at this point, the blazes disappear temporarily, so you need to be very vigilant. After passing a blaze on an old apple tree, you reach the edge of a field. Keep walking straight past the apple tree out into the field. There is an old fence line on your right, but most of the posts are long gone. However, about halfway across the field, you will spot a reassuring stake with a blue-blazed top. Follow the fence line as far as the trees on the far side of the field. There, blue blazes guide you sharp left around the edge of the field to a stile that takes you briefly back into woods.

The landscape is more pastoral over the final stretch; you pass through bush with rolling fields on your left. If you are feeling a bit hungry and you are there at the right time of the year, you will enjoy the raspberries and blackberries that grow by the side of the trail. Finally, a cart track takes you through light woodland back to the Duncan Crevice Caves Provincial Park to end a very satisfying walk.

For those who would like to complete the Duncan, Loree and Sly loops in one visit, there is no better place for an overnight stop than Bev and Ron Wren's Mountain Farm, high on the eastern shelf of the valley, north of Kimberley. The views over to the west rim and north to the bay are magnificent. It is not often that you find separate sleeping accommodations at a bed and breakfast, but the Wrens put up their guests in a self-contained cabin near to the farmhouse. It's a working sheep farm, so while you are there, buy some of Ron's lamb—it doesn't come much fresher.

The Loree Forest Loop

Trail Length: **4.4 kilometres**

Time: **2 hours**

Grade: **Moderate-strenuous**

Access: **From Grey County Road 2 at Victoria Corners, head east on 21-22 Sideroad for 5.2 kilometres.**

Map: ***Guide to the Bruce Trail:* map 24: Blue Mountain**

Parking: **On 21-22 Sideroad**

The Loree Forest Loop, with its dramatic views over both Georgian Bay and the Beaver Valley, was opened for hiking in September 1991, after more than five years of negotiations by the local Bruce Trail club with private and public landowners. The persistence of these volunteers has benefited all of us.

Where the 21-22 Sideroad swings east, look for the blue blazes on the

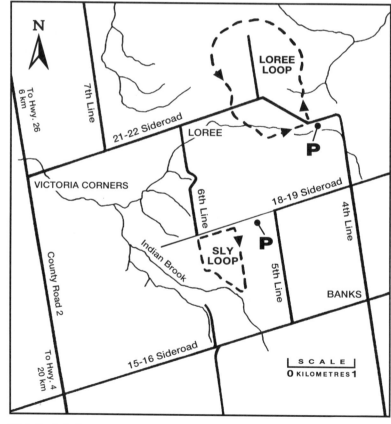

MAP 12B

north side of the road; a short connecting trail of about 200 metres heads north through an abandoned farm field. This route soon intersects the main Bruce Trail with its white blazes. Take the main trail to the left (west). For a while, the trail follows the edge of old pasture land, but soon descends steeply to a small stream valley. The usual trickle of water makes it hard to believe that this was the erosive force that carved out the gully.

After a small plateau where farm fields are now returning to forest, you climb a steep shale-covered slope. (This section is the only portion of the loop that could be called strenuous.) At the top, the trail turns left and levels out, hugging the valley's rim with its maple-birch forest and rich growth of ferns. It now begins a long arc, much of the time following an old cart track beside abandoned fields, to reach the top of the Georgian Peaks Ski Club property. On a clear day, the views are spectacular over the dark blue waters of Nottawasaga Bay. Sometimes, you can pick out Christian, Hope and Beckwith islands on the far horizon.

At the top of their slopes, the ski club warns it will prosecute anyone using mountain bikes or motorized vehicles on their land. Those of us who have seen the erosion damage such users cause will welcome this prohibition.

The trail next winds through mature maple woods along a path lined with crevices. In spring, the wildflowers are delightful; in fall, the coloured leaves can be spectacular. You cross an open field before returning to mixed woods. As the trail swings to the left, it comes out to a beautiful vista over the Beaver Valley.

From here, you drop down to the 21-22 Sideroad over hard-packed slopes where the topsoil has been washed away. Just before you get to the road, you come to a small stream. Be careful on its banks during wet weather; the clay can be very slippery.

The trail jogs east along the road for a very short distance before descending again to a small stream that is part of the Indian Brook watershed. On the south side of the stream, the trail follows the edge of several fields where cattle graze. Two stiles lead from field to field.

Just after a rather muddy crossing of another stream, the white-blazed main trail heads south on the 5th Line road allowance. From here, however, you take the blue-blazed allowance directly east for about 800 metres, crossing a bridge over a small creek. A bench is nearby for those who are getting weary. Soon you are back at your car.

Trail Length: **3.5 kilometres**

Time: **1.5 hours (with time to explore)**

Grade: **Moderate**

Access: **From the Loree parking spot, take 4th Line south for 1.3 kilometres. Turn west on 18-19 Sideroad.**

Map: ***Guide to the Bruce Trail:*** **map 24: Blue Mountain** *(see map on page 96)*

Parking: **On 18-19 Sideroad, just past the last farmhouse, before the road descends the escarpment**

The 3.5-kilometre Sly Trail is very close to the Loree Loop, and combining the two makes a very pleasant and varied half day on the trail. Park near a road sign warning drivers not to attempt the descent of the scarp, then walk down the hill and take the white-blazed trail to the left among the broken limestone. Watch out for the many entrances to what must be the largest groundhog home in the area!

After crossing some fields, you enter a wooded area where the trail wanders in a northwesterly direction along another tributary of the Indian Brook. It passes several beautiful waterfalls, at their best in the early spring when swollen by melting snow. Soon after, you will come across a delightful rock flowerpot, located in a small limestone bowl. This is a perfect spot for lunch.

Soon you meet the blue blazes of the Sly Side Trail, which swings north along the 6th Line road allowance. Turn right (east) at the 18-19 Sideroad to return to your car.

Until relatively recently, hiking in this beautiful upland area meant tedious tramping along hot and dusty side roads. Attractive loops for day-hiking were non-existent. The improvement is due to the unceasing efforts of the Beaver Valley Bruce Trail Club. Each reroute, each new piece of trail, demands forethought, negotiation and a lot of physical work, and we should all appreciate the efforts of the hard-working volunteers of the club. They have opened up to all of us some magnificent hiking country.

Beaver Valley Uplands

On Top of Old Baldy
Exploring the Beaver Valley

Trail Length: **14.7 kilometres**

Time: **6 hours**

Grade: **Strenuous**

Access: **From the south, from Highway 4 east of Flesherton, take County Road 13 north for 12.2 kilometres.**
From the north, from Highway 26 at Thornbury, take County Road 13 south for 25 kilometres.
Where County Road 13 meets County Road 7, turn east and head uphill on the unimproved 6-7 Sideroad. Drive for 1.5 kilometres to the top of the escarpment.

Map: ***Guide to the Bruce Trail:* map 25: Kimberley**

Parking: **Where 6-7 Sideroad swings left at the top of the escarpment, turn right into the Old Baldy Conservation Area parking lot.**

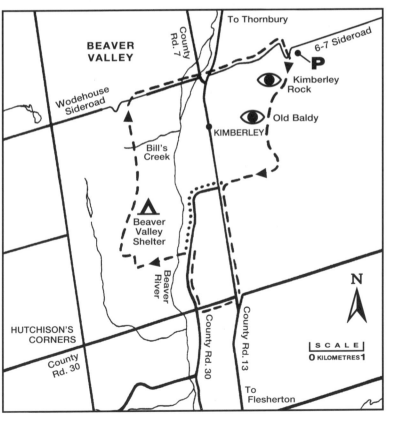

99   **MAP 13** **13**

Beaver Valley

Running from Highway 4 near Flesherton to the blue waters of Nottaw-asaga Bay, the Beaver Valley has a complex and compelling personality. Those who are familiar with its limestone crags, forested slopes, patch-work of fields and bountiful orchards know that here is a landscape of drama and variety.

You can catch an early hint of the drama if, on your way into the val-ley, you stop to look at Eugenia Falls. About 3.5 kilometres north of High-way 4, a sign directs you left into a conservation area. From the parking area, a short woodland path brings you out at a point overlooking the waterfall made by the Beaver River as it takes a 30-metre plunge over the sheer face of the escarpment.

When it was first discovered in 1853, a metallic glint of yellow beneath the rushing waters sparked a local gold rush. Alas, the metal was found to be worthless pyrite, fools' gold. But the falls' discovery did have its conse-quences; a town developed around dam sites that were built above the falls. It was named after the French Empress Eugenia, wife of Napoleon III, and its streets bore the names of the great battles of the Crimea.

Today, the bustling town has all but disappeared and the falls are much diminished, water having been largely diverted from Eugenia Lake through hydro flumes. But even so, this first brief glimpse of steep wood-ed slopes, sheer rock face and tumbled rock gives you a hint of the spec-tacular scenery that the valley has in store.

Yet no matter how well prepared you think you are, the first time you crest the hill above Kimberley, you will be surprised. Without warning, there it is, stretching out before you: to either side, high, steep, wooded valley walls with outcrops of sheer rock; below, farmsteads dotting the lower slopes, their green fields interspersed with small woodland groves; and down in the bottom of the valley, the Beaver River snaking its way to Thornbury and Nottawasaga Bay.

When you look at the size of the river, you know that it could not possi-bly have carved out a valley that is 24 kilometres long and almost 10 kilo-metres wide at its mouth. And indeed, it didn't. Like many of the valleys that slice through the escarpment, it was cut by a preglacial river and later scoured by glaciers into a broad-bottomed, deep-sided U-shape. On the upper slopes, a thin layer of till left by the glaciers provided just enough nourishment to allow hardy trees to survive, but lower down, where Lake Algonquin flooded the floor and lower slopes in the postglacial period, a thick mantle of silt and sand was left behind, forming nutrient-rich soils that today nourish some of Ontario's finest apple orchards.

From its first plummet over the escarpment at Eugenia Falls to its final plunge over the millrace at Thornbury, the Beaver River and its surround-ing countryside displays many different faces and has a myriad of trea-sures for the visitor to discover. There are many different ways to make these discoveries: walking, canoeing, bicycling and cross-country skiing are all popular modes. Obviously, our favourite is to explore on foot, and the walk described here, an elongated loop around Kimberley village, is a wonderful introduction to the valley.

Beaver Valley

13

Sorting the bumper crop, 1919.
– Credit: Ontario Ministry of Agriculture and Food, R.R. Sallows Collection

Starting from Old Baldy Conservation Area parking lot, the trail takes you south along the escarpment rim, descends part way to the valley, climbs south again and then drops west to the valley floor. After climbing the west slope, it takes you back northward. You complete the loop by returning back to your car along 6-7 Sideroad.

It is not a walk for the unfit or for the novice hiker. There are many steep ascents and descents, and for more than a third of the hike, you walk through open country with little shade. In summer, the sun can beat down unmercifully. The most gruelling bit is the walk at the end along 6-7 Sideroad. If your group has two cars, it is well worthwhile to park one on Wodehouse Sideroad, west of County Road 13. (Very little traffic passes along here so parking on the shoulder shouldn't pose a problem.) If you have only one car, an option is to park near the bottom of the valley and start the loop by walking up the east side of 6-7 Sideroad, then join the Bruce Trail as you pass through the Old Baldy parking area. This way, you do some of the road walking at the beginning while you are fresh.

You pick up the white blazes of the Bruce Trail in the parking area. The trail follows a fence line along the edge of a meadow and then passes through bush before entering the heavily wooded area along the escarpment edge. The path heads south, running very close to the cedar-lined edge and bringing you out at several spectacular lookouts along the way.

Without doubt, the most impressive vista is the one from the top of Old Baldy, 152 metres above the valley. On either side, massive cliffs rise up, studded here and there with stunted cedars. The rock surface, once scoured by glaciers, bears the scars of continuous weathering by water, ice and wind. Your downward glance passes first over the tops of trees, then beyond them to the hamlet of Kimberley and finally, further down, to the narrow valley floor with its winding ribbon of water. On the valley's western walls, no prominent cliffs extrude through the forest cover, but directly ahead, here and there, a ski run cuts a pale green swath through the darker green foliage. The contrast between stark cliffs and steep slopes at the top and the gentle, pastoral landscape of the valley floor makes this a compelling view.

When you are ready to tear yourself away, rejoin the trail and continue south. The path moves back from the edge a little and you find yourself walking through beautiful hardwoods. About .8 kilometres beyond Old Baldy, you reach a point where a steep, narrow valley cuts back into the cliff face. The trail descends here down a rocky and very steep path. It's not really difficult, but there is a bit of scrambling, so you need to take care, especially if the rocks are wet. The valley is a favourite haunt of turkey vultures and buteo hawks. As you descend, you will see them above, soaring on the updrafts created by the narrow valley walls, then suddenly swooping down to disappear from sight below you.

After climbing up the other side of the valley, you emerge onto an unopened road allowance, 3-4 Sideroad. The trail descends, first through trees, then open country, to meet County Road 13.

At this point, you have two options. The white blazes of the Bruce Trail will take you in a long curve, first south along County Road 13, then west through woodland and, finally, back north on County Road 30, along the bottom of the valley. The alternative is to cross over County Road 13 and follow County Road 30, first west, then south for about 1.5 kilometres, to meet the Bruce Trail coming from the opposite direction. Both options have their pros and cons. The Bruce Trail undoubtedly affords better views and also takes you through some pretty woods at the south end of the loop, but it also involves 2.7 kilometres of road walking, which can be hot and dusty. The other route takes you entirely by road but it is about 2.5 kilometres shorter.

If you decide to remain on the Bruce Trail, look for white blazes on the telephone poles on the east side of County Road 13. The road makes a gradual ascent up the valley. After about 1.3 kilometres, you come to the Beaver Valley Lookout on your right. If you feel like a rest, there are picnic tables and a splendid view of the valley and the river.

About .6 kilometres further on, the trail turns right, down what appears to be a private driveway. There are trees on your left at the turn. Don't head into the trees at the first blaze, but continue a few metres down the driveway to where the grass verge curves round. Here you will see a second blazed tree; enter the woods at this point.

The trail descends through the woods, at first quite steeply. You are following a fence line; trees give way to bush and overgrown meadow, and then, as you near the road (you will begin to hear traffic), trees close in again. The trail swings north and runs parallel to the road before emerging onto it directly opposite the rather grandiose entrance to the Beaver Valley Ski Club. You follow the road north for about 1.2 kilometres. Look for double blazes on a telephone pole on your right. Turn left opposite the blazes, into a laneway that takes you into Ministry of Natural Resources property. (If you are approaching from the north, by the shorter route, the double blazes will of course will be on your left; then turn right.)

After about 200 metres, you cross a bridge over the Beaver River, then after passing a barn and crossing a stile, head west across a large meadow. The last time we were there it was midsummer. The grass and waving heads of Queen Anne's lace were way above our heads and, of course, the blazes were invisible. Fortunately, the treadway was well marked.

Soon after it reaches the trees, the trail starts its abrupt climb up the escarpment. This is perhaps the most strenuous part of the walk, but the deep shade provided by tall trees means that the climb is relatively cool.

At the top, open, rolling countryside spreads out in front of you. A stile takes the trail to the right into a field. This is just about the halfway point in the walk, so you will probably be ready for lunch. If the weather is cool or overcast, you might want to carry on for a few minutes until you get to a lookout point, where you will get wonderful views, but no shade. If it is hot, you might prefer to stay right here.

In any event, before you cross the stile, walk a few metres south into the meadow that belongs to the Beaver Valley Ski Club. The view across

Thornbury Mills and the bridge over the Beaver River, circa 1908.
– Credit: County of Grey–Owen Sound Museum

the valley is magnificent; facing you, slightly to the left, are Old Baldy and Kimberley Rock, while a little to your right, on the edge of the rim, stand the tall towers of the Eugenia hydro plant. The hydro plant is the reason that Eugenia Falls is a mere shadow of its former self. Today, after eighty years of operation, most of the water of the upper Beaver River is still carried through wooden pipes from Lake Eugenia to turbines feeding two automated units, twenty-four hours a day, 365 days a year.

Beyond the stile, follow the edge of a field. The trees on your right thin out as you approach an old orchard; then you find yourself in open country. Wildflowers grow in wanton profusion along this high, sunny ridge. Sweet clover, in particular, runs rampant, its delicate pea-like flowers mingling with the brilliant blue of flax and salvia, the yellow of wild indigo and ranunculus and the purple of spotted knapweed. And time and again, along this open stretch of trail, you will get breathtaking vistas of the valley and opposite cliffs, and sometimes far beyond to the blue waters of Nottawasaga Bay.

The trail does not stay long in open country and the greater part of the journey along the west side of the valley takes you below the escarpment edge. Once it gets into trees, the trail makes a gradual descent, in twists and turns. The blazing is good, so you shouldn't have trouble. After about a kilometre, a blue-blazed trail goes off to the right across a bridge over a little stream. This leads to the Beaver Valley Shelter where you may camp overnight. You will encounter a number of other trails, most of them cross-country ski trails; ignore them and keep to the white-blazed route, which continues to head north.

About 1.3 kilometres north of the turnoff to the shelter, you will come to a bridge that crosses Bill's Creek. If you were to climb upstream a little way, you would find that the stream emerged from the hillside as a spring. It has its origins in Wodehouse Creek and rises in the till-covered uplands to the northwest. After flowing briefly east, then south, it disappears underground into sink holes (depressions in the rock caused by dolo-stone being dissolved by the acidity of rain water). Only during spring run-off does the creek flow overland; the rest of the year it vanishes below ground and reemerges in two springs on the west slope of the valley, one of them being Bill's Creek. This kind of underground drainage is known as a karst. Such features occur in a number of places along the escarpment, and the system here at Wodehouse is regarded as a particularly good example.

After crossing the creek you continue through trees for a further .5 kilometres before emerging into a more open landscape alternating between bush and field, with intermittent views over the valley. For some reason, the walk along the western slope always seems longer than it is. Perhaps the twisting path, rocky terrain and increasing fatigue have something to do with it. Anyhow, by the time you emerge from hardwood bush onto Wodehouse Sideroad, you may feel you have come a long way.

When you make your right turn onto the sideroad, you'll see the route stretching straight out into the valley and up the other side. If your car is parked not too far away, you will probably feel a sense of relief. Otherwise, the best that can be said about the 3-kilometre trek back to the Old Baldy parking area is that the road is very quiet and the journey somewhat enlivened by the wildflowers that line the route.

Once you cross the bottom of the valley, there is no shade, so be sure to have plenty of water to keep you going over this last bit, and rest assured that, once you get back to your car, the feeling of accomplishment makes it all worthwhile.

If you are tired, the hamlet of Kimberley, 1 kilometre south on County Road 13, makes a pleasant watering hole. Like many villages in and around the valley, it developed around a mill site. In the second half of the nineteenth century, Kimberley boasted two hotels, three blacksmiths and two carpenter's shops. Today, nineteenth-century bustle has been replaced by picturesque serenity. The visitor will find a general store, a couple of restaurants and some graceful old homes. For those who want a quiet weekend, there are several places to stay, and we can highly recommend Mary and Graham Lamont's guest home on a quiet side street in the middle of the village.

Beaver Valley

However, when you have recovered from your walk, if you want to explore more of the valley, drive north towards Nottawasaga Bay. It's a lovely journey; the valley floor broadens, the slopes become more gentle, and eventually, you find yourself passing through hectare after hectare of apple orchards.

The shelter afforded by the high ridge of the escarpment, together with the moderating influence of the waters of Georgian Bay, gives the northern part of the valley a longer and more reliable frost-free period than many areas further south. This climatic advantage combined with the rich, well-drained glacial soils, ideal for apple cultivation, has meant that the old mixed farms of the nineteenth century have been replaced by orchards. Apple trees are a pretty sight at any time, especially in spring when covered with millions of pink and white blossoms. But here in the Beaver Valley, the autumn, just before harvest, may be even lovelier. Ripe red apples hanging on the trees and the hillsides suffused by the glow of fall colours make an unforgettable impression.

As you approach the mouth of the river, you come to two more millsite villages, Clarksburg and Thornbury. When the railroad came to town, Thornbury flourished while Clarksburg became more of a backwater. Though it's hard to say where one ends and the other begins, Clarksburg, 3 kilometres upriver, is the smaller and quieter of the two. Either is a delightful spot for a weekend. In Clarksburg, Karen and Norm Stewart, owners of Hillside, a beautiful Victorian house, give hikers a warm welcome, charming accommodation and a wonderful breakfast. In Thornbury, Sally Pearson's Victorian house by the millpond is equally welcoming and comfortable.

Even if you don't want to stay overnight, Thornbury is worth a visit. The railway may be gone, but the town is anything but a ghost town. Of course, the lakeside site helps to make it attractive and so does the long stretch of public parkland adjacent to the shore. And the town boasts some lovely old houses, some modest, some rather splendid. Its traditional main street, complete with butcher and baker (we're not sure about a candlestick maker), bustles with life, and there are a number of good places to eat. Perhaps the most attractive is by the dam, where the old mill is now enjoying a reincarnation as the Mill Café. On a hot summer's evening you can sit out on the terrace and watch the water flow over the dam while you eat locally caught trout.

Thornbury makes a good base for a number of walks. The upland areas of Kolapore, Duncan and Loree are virtually on the doorstep, and the Blue Mountains and Pretty River loops are easily reached. And after clambering among cliffs and crevices, what could be better than to end the day on the tranquil shore where the Beaver River completes its journey and merges with the waters of Nottawasaga Bay?

N.B. Just as we went to press we heard that a section of trail south of Old Baldy was about to be closed. For details of a reroute call the BTA at 1-800-665-HIKE. Remember that blazes always take precedence over hike descriptions.

Three Rivers and a Hidden Glen
Exploring Inglis Falls and The Glen

Inglis Falls, probably late 1860s, showing the mill buildings in the background.
– Credit: County of Grey–Owen Sound Museum

The sparkling blue waters of Georgian Bay beckon visitors to Owen Sound, which markets itself as "the Scenic City." Part of its attractiveness comes from the beautiful rivers that make their way over the escarpment and flow through Owen Sound's harbour into Georgian Bay. To the south, the Sydenham River makes a spectacular descent over Inglis Falls, then meanders peacefully through Harrison Park and past stately Victorian homes. A little further west, the Pottawatami River tumbles over Jones Falls on its final journey to the bay. From the conservation areas that surround both of these falls, you can undertake numerous walks, and although you are never more than 3 kilometres from the city centre, lookouts allow you to peer into deep gorges, and trails take you to the site of an old mill, and past fly fishermen attempting to pluck trout or salmon from the river.

A little further afield is another river, Indian Creek, which makes a dramatic final plunge into the waters of the bay, 5 kilometres north of the city. Here again, there are pleasant walks through conservation lands. This third river is the one that leads to the hidden glen. A few kilometres upstream, just past the point where Mud Creek swings southeast to join Indian Creek, is a hiker's and naturalist's paradise—one of the secret treasures of the Bruce Trail.

Inglis Falls and Harrison Park

Trail Length: **7 kilometres**

Time: **3 hours**

Grade: **Moderate**

Access: **From Rockford, on Highway 6 just south of Owen Sound, turn left onto County Road 18 and go west for 1.4 kilometres. Then proceed north on Inglis Falls Road for 500 metres to the entrance to the conservation area.**

Map: **Guide to the Bruce Trail: map 30: Inglis Falls. A detailed map is available from the information centre beside the falls.**

Parking: **There is a parking area next to the falls.**

The highlight for any hiker's visit to the area is the Inglis Falls Conservation Area. It stands just to the west of Rockford and Highway 6; signs direct you easily to the parking area just above the falls.

You will immediately see two millstones, relics of a bygone era when grist and saw mills stood on this site. For ninety years, from 1845 to 1934, the Inglis family harnessed the power of the falls. After the Inglis's era, the mills continued under new owners until 1945 when fire destroyed them, ending a century of pioneer industrial history.

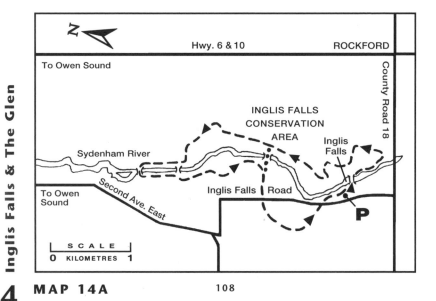

Inglis Falls & The Glen

14 **MAP 14A** 108

*Three ladies cool off in the river at Patterson House Park
(now Harrison Park)*
– Credit: County of Grey–Owen Sound Museum

If you take the bridge across the Sydenham River to the old stable that is now an information centre, you can learn the story of Peter Inglis. Born in a small village in Scotland in 1813, the second youngest in a family of nine, he emigrated to Canada in 1845 at the age of thirty-two. He bought the falls and the grist mill, which had been built three years earlier, and then married Ann Carroll, a native of Ireland; together they raised seven children.

Inglis Falls was the site of one of the earliest mill complexes in the northern section of the escarpment, and it is remarkable that the area has been preserved. You can see the remains of the original structure below the falls. In the mill's early years, oxen teams came from as far as Collingwood and Mount Forest.

As business grew, the budding entrepreneur developed a flour mill, a woollen mill and a sawmill at the site. In 1862, Inglis replaced the original grist mill with a larger four-storey building. He produced a variety of brands of flour and bran and an animal feed called shorts. His woollen mill, twice burned and rebuilt, was noted for its splendid blankets. Today, it is mainly the memories of this pioneer venture that remain.

From the information centre, follow the white blazes of the Bruce Trail upstream (south) along the river and into the cedars. The weir that stored water for the long-vanished mill still stands. The trail here is well blazed and signed, and the treadway has been built up with stone chips. It loops out towards Highway 6 and then back, and in winter, creates a pleasant cross-country ski track.

After .5 kilometres, however, turn left and follow the conservation authority signs to Harrison Park. You pass a number of Trail Closed signs, where the staff are trying to regenerate vegetation destroyed along unauthorized routes. Soon the trail descends through a narrow cleft in the scarp. Although it is not dangerous in the summer, be warned that this is an expert cross-country ski trail; do not attempt it in winter without considerable experience!

Soon you hear the sounds of the river as it tumbles over rocks and boulders. The trail now follows the east bank of the river and can be muddy; the conservation authority, however, has built some excellent walkways. If you feel like taking things easy, there are the remains of another mill to look at, and the attempts of fly fisherman may provide an interesting diversion.

After 2.3 kilometres, you come to a signpost where you will have to make a decision. If time or energy is a problem, turn left and cross the bridge over the river to the administration centre. However, we recommend that you take the trail to the right, up the hill and on to Harrison Park. The route leads into pine reforestation. If you look back, you will see the exposed scarp edge on the east side of the valley. In July and August, stop to feast on the blackberries and raspberries that are reclaiming the abandoned farm fields.

The trail drops sharply into mature woods at the south end of Harrison Park. Near the heart of the city, this beautiful area of more than 40 hectares lines the banks of the Sydenham River. It is a delightful urban oasis with tennis courts, wading and swimming pools, several playgrounds, a fully equipped campground and picnic areas. Also, a picturesque inn offers relaxed dining for those who appreciate the finer touches. A variety of walking and ski trails make the park a popular attraction for all ages, through all seasons. A waterfowl area is home to ducks, Canada geese and other species.

Walk downstream along the east bank of the river and circle past the inn; then return upstream on the west side through the crowded but clean campground. At the south end of Harrison Park, you leave Mile Drive, which has circled through the park; the footpath now enters a reforested area. Stay between the stakes (as the sign indicates) to allow the vegetation to regenerate. Then at the fork in the trail, take the left branch up the hill and towards the river. Again, you have good views of the exposed scarp. You cross farm fields and then drop into a mature woods where the path can be muddy. Soon you join the trail from the bridge over the river; this would have been your route if you had taken the shorter alternative omitting Harrison Park. You now turn right to join this path, leading away from the river and past the workshops to the arboretum.

Walk through the arboretum to its southwest corner and exit onto the Inglis Falls Road. Head south along the road for a short distance and then cross to the west side where the forest meets the farm field. Head west for about 50 metres and watch carefully at the corner of the field where the trail enters the woods. Used primarily as a ski trail, this route is not as well signed. It heads up the scarp; where the bush road ends, it turns right and then left on an old logging track, which may be overgrown. Soon, however, you meet the Bruce Trail and its white blazing; turn left towards Inglis Falls. The route heads through a thick maple bush before crossing into the open fields to the south. Soon you again reach the Inglis Falls Road, close to your car.

The most spectacular view is still to come. Follow the rough trail over the limestone blocks at the edge of the gorge and stay behind the protective wall. (In 1992, a tourist who ventured too close died from a fall to the rocks below.) The lookouts will no doubt be the highlight of your hike. This breathtaking falls cascades over an 18-metre cliff, down into the steep gorge that has been carved out by the force of the falling water. The panoramic view is unforgettable.

This vista has always been a source of pride for residents of the Scenic City. Andrew Armitage, in *Owen Sound: The Day The Governor General Came To Town and Other Tales,* recounts the visit on July 30, 1874, of Lord and Lady Dufferin. A welcoming committee had spent hundreds of hours planning for this day, and the crowning event was to be a sightseeing tour of Inglis Falls, the "Niagara of the North."

The problem, however, was the season: in mid-summer the Sydenham poured over the falls, not with a mighty roar, but with a mere trickle. But the mayor and his committee were determined to solve the problem.

By the afternoon of July 30, all was ready. Drawn by four matched horses, a special carriage brought the regal couple towards the falls. As they stepped out onto the mill road, they heard a mighty roar of water. Accompanied by Peter Inglis, the party walked to the edge of the precipice, stood on the jutting rocks and exclaimed on the mighty works of nature and of God. For there, surrounding the Inglis Mill, was an absolute torrent of water rushing down the gorge!

The thousands of Owen Sounders who had followed the procession were amazed; never had they seen such a mighty river of water over the falls, not even during spring run-off. But there had been rumours throughout the community.

As Lord Dufferin paused to examine the workings of the mill, the mayor became agitated and ushered the dignitaries swiftly to their carriage. Only the last stragglers noted that the rush of water had by now shrunk to the normal July trickle.

The secret was not hidden for long. For weeks, a group of townsmen and farmers had been working in secret to build a coffer dam above the falls ∧ great reservoir of water backed up, awaiting the right moment. As the governor general was driven to the edge of the falls, the gates were pulled and the stored waters rushed forward. Of course, the limited reserves meant that the spectacle was short-lived, and the dignitaries had to be rushed on their way. But that night, the residents of Owen Sound basked in the afterglow of a successful regal visit!

The other waterfalls in the area are certainly worth a visit. From Inglis Falls, drive north and turn left along County Road 5. Turn north on County Road 18 and after 3 kilometres, you will see the Pottawatomi Conservation Area at the junction of highways 6, 21 and 70. From the parking area by the Grey-Bruce Tourist Association office, take the hiking trail that crosses over a small stream. When the path links up with the white blazes of the Bruce Trail, follow it north to a lookout. From the prominent escarpment face, there is a magnificent view of the surrounding lowlands and scenic Jones Falls. Here the Pottawatomi River cascades 12 metres over the scarp edge on its way to Owen Sound. The river below the falls is teaming with life. Rainbow trout and coho salmon use this spot as a spawning ground, and both brown trout and splake feed here. From the lookout, you can follow the Bruce Trail further along the escarpment or hike along the trail system of the conservation area.

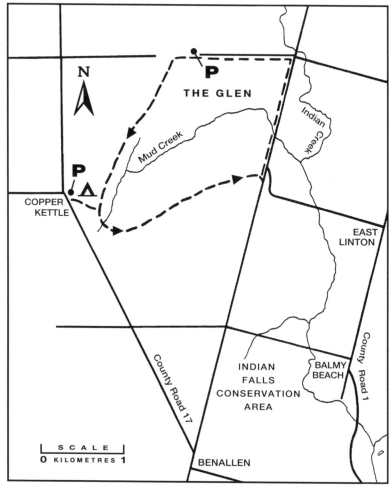

Inglis Falls & The Glen

N

THE GLEN

Indian Creek

Mud Creek

P

COPPER KETTLE

EAST LINTON

County Road 17

INDIAN FALLS CONSERVATION AREA

BALMY BEACH

County Road 1

SCALE
0 KILOMETRES 1

BENALLEN

MAP 14B

Indian Falls is 5 kilometres north of Owen Sound on Grey County Road 1. The 15-metre horseshoe-shaped waterfall got its name from the Nawash Indians who formerly lived here. If you walk along the .8-kilometre trail, you get good views of the falls and the creek bed. The conservation area also has a children's playground, picnic tables and several sports areas developed by the Township of Sarawak.

The Glen

Trail Length: **11.2 kilometres**

Time: **5–6 hours**

Grade: **Moderate-strenuous**

Access: **From downtown Owen Sound, take Grey County Road 1 (which starts out as Second Avenue West at highways 6 and 21) north for 5 kilometres to County Road 17. Follow it west and north about 4 kilometres beyond Benallen.**

Map: ***Guide to the Bruce Trail:* map 31: Owen Sound**

Parking: **A gravel parking area is located on the east side of Grey County Road 17, just south of the hamlet of Copper Kettle.**

About 550 metres southeast along the county road from the parking area, you will find a blue-blazed forest track, which provides an easy 500-metre link to the main trail. At the spot where the two meet, there is a wilderness campsite. Just 75 metres to the north, a perpetually flowing spring, the headwaters of Mud Creek, bubbles up from the limestone at a point just below the trail. (As always along the escarpment, remember to boil or treat the water.) Begin by heading south and east in a counter-clockwise direction on the main trail. Soon the path crosses some dramatic crevices as it hugs the escarpment edge. The cliffs on which you stand are the result of wave action; they were part of the shoreline of Lake Algonquin, the huge forerunner of Lakes Huron and Michigan, formed by the melting of glacial ice. From the cliffs, there are some great vistas across The Glen to the north and west, over a sea of trees. On a fall day, the view over the colourful hardwoods to the blue waters of Georgian Bay can be spectacular. The Glen area today is a swampy wilderness, the wetlands a relic of the higher water levels of postglacial times. Now, only the headwaters of Mud Creek remain, crossing over lands that have always been too wet to farm successfully.

After 2.9 kilometres, just past an abandoned field, the main trail swings to the south into a maple woods and a blue trail heads north on an extremely rough path down the escarpment. Watch carefully for the blazes. This is the route that has just been reopened; the blazes exist but, until you reach the road, the treadway is not evident and the route is entangled with vegetation. The struggle lasts only a hundred metres, however; then you head north for 1.8 kilometres on the Kepple-Sarawak Townline.

Inglis Falls & The Glen

Take the first side road to the left (west) for 1.4 kilometres to its end. (Note: The roads are not blazed.) From this point, there is some rough scrambling for 200 metres. The blue-blazed route swings south for a short distance along the swamp, crosses west on the north side of the fence line and then climbs dramatically up a crevice to the top of the scarp. Again, because the route is new and as yet little used, the path is not always clear, but it will improve as more people discover it.

At the top, turn left for the climax of the hike. For approximately one hour, you traverse some dramatic country. On the left, the cliffs gradually increase in height, and deep crevices cut across the trail. Standing rocks tempt you to explore below the scarp edge, but never try such a scramble alone, the potential dangers are too great.

The plant life is magnificent. Several years ago, an Owen Sound company marketed sweat shirts encouraging you to hike the Bruce Trail "just for the fern of it," and walking along here, you can see why. The rock faces of the escarpment and the cool shaded woodlands on its lower slopes in this area are home to the largest variety of ferns in the province. The rich greens of the walking fern, hart's tongue and maidenhair abound in the cool moist crevices. Orchids such as rattlesnake plantain grow right beside the trail. Amid the cedars at the scarp edge, you will see huge white pine stumps—relics of logging that took place a century ago. All too soon, you are back at the campsite and the short trek to your car.

If you have time, you can do two other short hikes. Fifty metres south of the campsite, an old cart track leads down the scarp to the floor of The Glen. In the fall, amid the pine reforestation and the abandoned farm fields, you'll find yourself surrounded by a riot of colour: the purple of asters, the yellow of goldenrod and the white of Queen Anne's lace.

On the west side of the County Road across from the parking area, a 2-kilometre conservation authority trail lets you explore a spectacular bog. Be warned, however, that the trail will be wet, and a number of deadfalls will block the path. This is also a seldom-travelled route and it's easy to become lost; never hike it alone. But the wildflowers, abundant bird life, and beaver activity make it a rich experience for a naturalist.

The area of The Glen is enticing, both for its beauty and its isolation. You will be tempted to return; its resources are too rich to digest in an introductory visit.

Owen Sound is a beautiful city, and those who want to stay for a while will find plenty to see and do and good accommodation to choose from. However, if you prefer to stay somewhere a little more secluded, try Hollyhock Acres, near Chatsworth, about 10 kilometres south of Owen Sound. Bette and Barry Lewin's century-old farmhouse sits on 301 hectares of rolling land. The hearty breakfast (in summer served on the deck overlooking a pond) will set you up for the day, and after a hard day's walking, you can recover in the outdoor hot tub. If it sounds like total bliss, it is!

The Treasures of Colpoy's Bay
The Escarpment Parks of the Wiarton Area

The barge Thos. R. Scott *and the tug* Crawford *moored below the escarpment cliffs at Wiarton, circa 1911.*
– Credit: County of Bruce Museum

In 1985, amid a great deal of controversy and after nearly eighteen years of study, the Ontario government with the support of all three political parties approved the Niagara Escarpment Plan. The first of its kind in Ontario, the plan was designed to control the quantity and quality of development along the escarpment.

One of its provisions was a system of 105 parks designed to protect distinctive features and to provide access to important natural areas. A twenty-five-million-dollar, ten-year program was begun to acquire land for this system and for a trail corridor that would connect these parks. Hikers rejoiced at the naming of the Bruce Trail as "an essential component of the Niagara Escarpment Parks System linking parks and natural features."

Colpoy's Bay

15

The plan divided the escarpment into ten segments and, to each, assigned a principal park. The intent was to build interpretive centres to educate the public on a wide range of topics such as geology, flora and fauna, and local history.

Near Wiarton, there are four parks that offer day-hiking possibilities. They offer a guarantee that the area's unique natural features and the magnificent vistas over the waters of Colpoy's Bay are permanently protected. The hikes described here take you to all four of these parks. Each has its own unique features; each is spectacular in its own way; and together they take you on a fascinating exploration of the treasures of Colpoy's Bay.

Skinner's Bluff Conservation Area

Trail Length: **15.6 kilometres (long loop) or 8.5 kilometres (short loop)**

Time: **5–6 hours or 2.5–3 hours**

Grade: **Easy, except for the length of the longer loop**

Access: **From Wiarton, take Island View Drive (Grey County Road 26) east for 4 kilometres to Oxenden, then 900 metres further east to where a sign directs you to the Bruce's Caves Conservation Area parking lot, a further 1 kilometre down a dirt road.**

Map: **Guide to the Bruce Trail: map 33: Wiarton**

Parking: **At the Bruce's Caves Conservation Area**

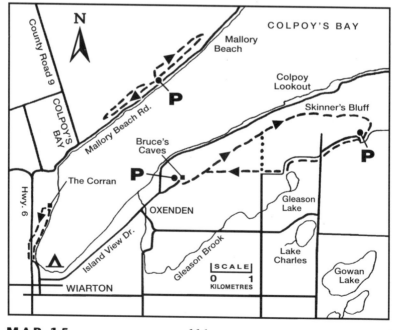

Skinner's Bluff Conservation Area, on the top of the escarpment above the south shore of Colpoy's Bay, is a principal park. As yet undeveloped, it provides the hiker with relatively easy footpaths into the heart of escarpment country.

From the parking lot at the Bruce's Caves Conservation Area, a good trail leads to the top of the escarpment. The white blazes then turn left on an old logging track. The terrain makes for easy hiking through a young second-growth maple bush that is especially colourful in the fall.

After about a kilometre, you come to a large boulder to the right of the trail. This is an erratic, a chunk of rock from the Canadian Shield that was pried loose by a glacier, carried along its southward course and then deposited here. Just beyond, the trail forks. Straight ahead is the blue-blazed trail on which you will return. For now, turn left and follow the white blazes as they head out towards Skinner's Bluff.

After 2.5 kilometres of easy hiking, you come to blue blazes on two beech trees, indicating a turn to the south. If you prefer a shorter walk, take this route, and when you reach Gleason Lake Road, turn right (or west) to return along another blue-blazed road allowance towards the parking lot. This makes an 8.5-kilometre loop, which may be preferable for those without the stamina to complete the full route. However, you have yet to see the magnificent lookouts over the water, so if time and weather permit, the longer loop is well worth the effort.

In approximately 1 kilometre, the trail approaches the escarpment edge. At first, there are only tantalizing glimpses through the trees, but then you reach the first of a series of lookouts. Below you are the old farms carved out from what was formerly the lake bottom when postglacial water levels were much higher. Across the bay are the cottages of Mallory Beach and the gleaming white cliffs of Malcolm Bluff.

For the next 4 kilometres, the trail follows the scarp. Although not difficult hiking, the footing is somewhat rougher. Inland from the trail are occasional farm fields. In the height of summer you will be walking through waist-high grasses and white-topped Queen Anne's lace. From a series of lookouts, you look down on the sails of tiny boats skimming over the water, the islands at the mouth of Colpoy's Bay, and, in the distance, the peninsula of Cape Croker reaching far out into Georgian Bay.

As you approach the eastern end of Skinner's Bluff, the trail swings to the south and enters a more mature woods. From the last of the lookouts (incidentally, a great place for a lunch break), if you look to the southeast, you get a vivid sense of what the Georgian Bay shoreline looked like 11,500 years ago.

At that time, most of Southern Ontario was covered by a huge lake, known as proglacial Lake Algonquin. The retreating ice formed its north shore—hence the term proglacial, in front of the ice. The lake occupied the Michigan-Huron and the Georgian Bay basins. Skinner's Bluff, where you are standing, was part of the Lake Algonquin shoreline, one of a number of promontories that jutted out into the lake. To the southeast, you can see another, Esther's Bluff, and behind it, on the other side of what used to be a deep bay (now the Slough of Despond), is a third promontory, Halliday Hill. (If the faces of the cliffs remind you of those of The Glen, further south towards Owen Sound, it is because they too were once part of the old shoreline.)

After the lookout, the trail soon descends to a dirt road. Leave the white blazes at this point and follow the road to the right (west). Although we usually have an intense dislike for hiking along dusty roads, this is a pleasant single lane leading past Skinner's Bluff Farm. Your chances of meeting traffic are very slim.

At the Yield sign, turn left (south) and, after only 20 metres or so, turn right (west) on a single track that is even less used. It heads west and then south and then west again past Gleason Lake, a shallow body of water perched close to the escarpment edge. Opportunities for bird-watching abound.

After a total of 3.5 kilometres of road walking, the Gleason Lake Road turns sharply left (south). Here is the junction of two blue-blazed trails. One comes from the north and is the route you would have hiked if you had chosen the shorter 8.5-kilometre loop. The other heads west on a well-cleared logging track to lead you back towards your car. Along the path, the flat limestone pavement indicates all too clearly why farming failed close to the escarpment edge. After about 2 kilometres of easy walking, you are back at the white blazes of the main trail where the large erratic marks the trail junction. From here, it is a short journey back to the parking lot.

Bruce's Caves Conservation Area is a small park. It is best to leave it until after the Skinner's Bluff hike. From the parking lot, a well-maintained short trail leads to the caves, which dramatically illustrate ancient weathering processes and the levels of Lake Algonquin. Pebbles and boulders were picked up by waves that continually pounded away at the cliff face; slabs of rock broke away, and eventually, hollow caverns developed.

The most prominent cave has an enormous central pillar flanked by two arched entrances. The hollow formed by the waves was enlarged by surface and ground water that worked along the joints and lines of stratification, dissolving the soluble limestone. The softer layers beneath the dolostone cap-rock were eroded, frequently breaking off. Today, the floor of the caves is littered with the resulting slabs of rock. In addition, further along the scarp, large sections of rock have sheared off the cliff face, creating long narrow crevices and caves. On the rocky slopes below the caves, you find characteristic escarpment vegetation, including rock ferns such as polypody, walking fern and slender cliff-brake.

The caves' name, by the way, came from an eccentric hermit named Bruce, a British remittance man who owned the cave property a hundred years ago. He lived in a small shanty near the entrance and charged a minimal fee to the numerous tourists who came by horse and buggy to view the caves. The mode of transportation may have changed, but the public's curiosity is just as strong. After the peacefulness of the Skinner's Bluff loop, you will struck by the increase in the number of people.

Wiarton–Spirit Rock Loop

Trail Length:	**5.3 kilometres**
Time:	**2 hours**
Grade:	**Easy**
Access:	**From Wiarton, take Highway 6. Follow the signs to Spirit Rock Conservation Area just north of the town.**
Map:	**Guide to the Bruce Trail: map 33: Wiarton** (*see map on page 116*)
Parking:	**Near the Corran at Spirit Rock Conservation Area**

Spirit Rock Conservation Area attracts visitors interested in local history, in its legends, and in the remarkable view over Colpoy's Bay. Your first encounter will be with history.

In 1881, this site became the home of Alexander McNeil, who developed an estate of beautiful gardens, well-kept lawns and productive orchards. Its heart was the Corran, a seventeen-room mansion, lavish with oriental carvings, ancient weapons, tapestries and book-lined walls. McNeil's mansion was modelled and named after his childhood home in Northern Ireland. The Gaelic meaning of corran is "point of land running into the sea."

McNeil was known for his extravagant parties for members of parliament and other leading figures. On departure, every guest received a single rose, picked from one of the five hundred rose bushes in the 7-hectare gardens.

In the same year the Corran was built, McNeil became the federal member of parliament for the North Bruce riding, a position he held for twenty years. He died in 1932 at the age of ninety, and his son inherited the estate. As so often happens, the second generation did not have the same talents or commitment; the estate quickly deteriorated, the family fortune dwindled away, and the property was vandalized. In the 1960s, it was sold to the conservation authority. Soon the house burned, leaving only the stone shell that you see today. It remains a haunting presence.

From the Corran, a 5.3-kilometre loop trail leads into Wiarton and then back to the conservation authority parking lot. Take the spiral staircase down the face of the escarpment to the shores of Colpoy's Bay. There, follow the white blazes of the Bruce Trail to the right through the cedars just above the boulder beach. Soon you pass the Wiarton Water Treatment Plant, completed in 1993, and a large marina. To the right is Spirit Rock, for which the conservation area is named.

The legend of Spirit Rock is similar to the one that accounts for the flowerpot formations at the northern tip of the Bruce. An Indian maiden fell in love with a chief from an enemy tribe, and her family turned against her. In despair, she threw herself over the cliff. Today, when the lighting and angles are just right, the face of the maiden can supposedly be seen in the cliffs from below.

The white blazes continue along the road towards downtown. At Divi-

Colpoy's Bay

sion Street, the loop turns right, following blue blazes and ascending the escarpment via Highway 6. At the top, it enters a private driveway and soon bears left into the bush and the conservation authority property. There it follows the blazes along a ski trail back to the parking area by the Corran.

Colpoy's Bluff Side Trail

Trail Length: **7.3 kilometres**

Time: **3 hours**

Grade: **Moderate**

Access: **From Wiarton, take Highway 6 for 2 kilometres and then turn east on Bruce County Road 9 to the community of Colpoy's Bay. From here take Mallory Beach Road east for 3 kilometres to an S-bend in the road. At the bend, turn left and go 100 metres to where the road dead-ends.**

Map: **Guide to the Bruce Trail: maps 33 and 34: Wiarton and Cape Croker (see map on page 116)**

Parking: **Near the turning circle where the road ends**

The village of Colpoy's Bay is a nineteenth-century fishing and logging community whose population once outnumbered Wiarton's. Now the pilings from the old docks are the most obvious reminder of a bygone era.

From the parking area 3 kilometres east of the village, return east on foot to the S-bend and take the road allowance up the escarpment between two homes. In pioneer days, this path was a logging track where timber was dragged down from the scarp to be floated to the mills in the bay.

The Colpoy's Bluff Side Trail loop is 7.3 kilometres long. At the top of the escarpment, head west on the white-blazed main trail. After 1.3 kilometres, the trail curves inland to meet a forest access road. Here turn right (east) on the blue-blazed track, which continues for 3.5 kilometres through pleasant woods.

The blue blazes lead eventually to the main trail; turn right and follow the white blazes back for 2.5 kilometres to return to the trail by which you first ascended the scarp. This section is much more demanding, but the spectacular views amply compensate.

On the far side of the bay, you can see the dramatic heights of Skinner's Bluff. If you have done all the loops, then this view of your starting point makes a fitting climax to a hiking holiday above the shores of Colpoy's Bay.

Each of these four parks has its own special charm but together they serve a common objective: to preserve the Niagara Escarpment and open it to public recreation. To some, in this day of large government deficits, the land acquisition program may seem folly, but generations to come will praise the wisdom of their elders for preserving one of the world's unique ecological environments.

Colpoy's Bay

120

The Challenge of the Bruce
The Trails of Gun Point

Trail Length: **16 kilometres**

Time: **Allow a minimum of 6 hours. The loop is also an excellent weekend's backpacking adventure.**

Grade: **Strenuous**

Access: **From Bruce County Road 9, just north of Barrow Bay, shortly after the road turns to the west, take the gravel track on the right. It heads north for 300 metres to a T-intersection where you turn right and head east to the turning circle at the end of the road.**

Map: ***Guide to the Bruce Trail:* map 36: Lion's Head**

Parking: **Park at the turning circle beside the sign indicating the Lion's Head Provincial Nature Reserve.**

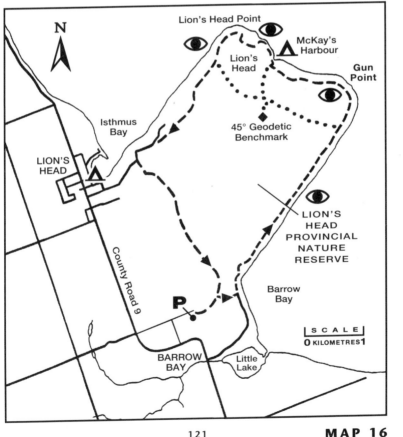

N

Lion's Head Point

McKay's Harbour

Lion's Head

Gun Point

Isthmus Bay

45° Geodetic Benchmark

LION'S HEAD

LION'S HEAD PROVINCIAL NATURE RESERVE

County Road 9

P

Barrow Bay

SCALE
0 KILOMETRES 1

BARROW BAY

Little Lake

Gun Point

MAP 16

16

Between Barrow Bay and Lion's Head, a spectacular peninsula juts out into the open waters of Georgian Bay. Until the mid 1980s, it was largely inaccessible to the hiker. The Bruce Trail cut across the neck, mainly on old logging roads, but there was no trail around the perimeter or through the body of the peninsula. Now, thanks to the cooperation of the local Ministry of Natural Resources staff and the volunteer trail builders of the Bruce Trail Association, the peninsula can be explored on a hiking loop that takes in some of the most beautiful vistas along the entire Bruce Trail. The lookouts from both Gun Point and the Lion's Head are truly exceptional.

It is not an adventure for the inexperienced; it is without question the most difficult hike described in this book. Yet it is a unique journey into an area that was heavily logged at the turn of the century and since then has seen minimal human activity. It is as close to a true wilderness experience as you will find on the Bruce.

From the parking area, follow the cart track and its yellow blazes, which lead to the Ilse Hanel Side Trail. The blue-blazed side trail to the left was the original route of the Bruce Trail, and it is the route by which you will later return to complete the loop.

An unknown bowler-hatted man stands on a
natural rock bridge near Lion's Head.
– Credit: County of Grey–Owen Sound Museum

16

At this junction, follow the blue blazes straight ahead across the meadow and over a ridge into the woods. In less than a kilometre you will meet the white blazes of today's Bruce Trail coming in from the right at the end of the Barrow Bay North Cottage Road. (Please note: There is no parking allowed on this road.)

For the next 5 kilometres to Gun Point, you follow the rugged edge of the escarpment over the tumbled limestone. From the many lookouts, you can see the cottages in the curve of Barrow Bay on your right and the cliffs near Rush Cove on the far shore. Further along, the Cape Dundas headland juts out into the water towards Barrier Island, and beyond that looms the outline of Cape Croker.

Just before Gun Point is the Inland Trail, which provides an alternative to the main route. But unless the weather is really bad, continue on to the point. The last 400 metres is especially attractive as the vegetation thins out and the trail hugs the open edge of the cliffs. Below, you can see the recent rock falls, a reminder that erosion is a never-ending process and that the escarpment face is continually changing under the assault of the elements.

After Gun Point, the trail swings to the left. More lookouts follow: below you, on the shore of the peninsula, nestles McKay's Harbour; across the wide curve of Isthmus Bay, you can see the promontories of White Bluff, Smokey Head and Cape Chin and, much further off, the broad headland of Cabot Head.

After about 2 kilometres, the escarpment edge breaks down to a steep valley created thousands of years ago by glacial run-off. The trail descends a hill, runs along the base of a small rock face and then drops once again to reach an old logging track. Turn right and follow the white blazes; to the left is a yellow-blazed side trail leading back to the Inland Trail.

After about 300 metres, you come out onto a sandy beach called Mc-Kay's Harbour. The area was named after Captain John McKay, one of the pioneer settlers of Lion's Head. Walter Warder, in his history of the area, describes McKay as "a familiar figure here, a lover of the waters, a good tug captain who could handle well any kind of fishing boat." McKay was an ardent fisherman and even had his own harbour, a channel dug by his own labour that provided a haven for his fishing boat, safe from wind and sea. Here he raised a large, seafaring family; four of his sons grew up to be captains of boats on the Great Lakes.

Then on November 9, 1913, the area was besieged by one of those ferocious fall storms that have always plagued Great Lakes shipping. The hurricane-force winds destroyed McKay's channel and obliterated the harbour. Today, all that is left is a wilderness cove; nature has eradicated any sign of previous settlement.

McKay's Harbour offers superb wilderness camping for the backpacker. A small number of tents can be pitched by the beach. If storms or high water are flooding the camping area, it is possible to set up a tent in the woods on the first plateau above the beach. As well, McKay's Harbour is the only source of drinking water on the whole loop. (Remember that water from the bay should be treated or boiled.)

You are urged to be especially careful to leave no signs of your presence in this special place. (A small latrine is located off the first plateau.) Because of its beauty, the area receives heavy use. Only with the cooperation of all of us and by practising a no-trace camping ethic can its beauty be preserved.

From the campsite, the trail continues along the beach past a beaver pond. After 500 metres, you reach a broad area of ancient cobblestone terraces, a product of the changing water levels of Georgian Bay since the last glaciation.

From here, the path turns inland and crosses a rocky plateau. At first, you will pass through stunted trees, their height sacrificed in the struggle to survive in an inhospitable environment, but then you enter denser forest. Watch out for the heavy growth of poison ivy on the beach terraces and the plateau; poison ivy thrives best where little else will grow.

When you reach the base of the escarpment, the trail climbs past a huge boulder and beneath an impressive hanging ledge. At the top, you follow the escarpment edge as it gradually curves left. The next 2 kilometres to the lookout is difficult walking; be especially careful during wet weather, when the consequences of a slip could be disastrous.

Next you reach the lookout with one of the most impressive vistas along the entire 780 kilometres of the Bruce Trail. You are standing on an outlier, set off from the escarpment walls. The views in both directions along the shoreline are stunning. To the left is the harbour and village of Lion's Head, and directly across the bay are the towering cliffs of White Bluff. You are standing on top of the Lion's Head, and below you is a sheer drop to where the waves pound on the rocky shore.

Within 100 metres, you will meet the blue blazes of the Inland Trail coming in on your left to rejoin the main trail. Continue to follow the white blazes as they lead southwesterly through cedars and among the rough limestone outcroppings. After about a kilometre, near the edge, the trail swings inland and becomes much easier.

When you come to a point where the trail passes between two rocky outcrops, a short side trail to the left leads to an interesting chimneylike formation. It is another intriguing geological reminder of the escarpment's past history when great glacial rivers covered much of the land. Thought to be formed on a river bed by the action of the current and swirling stones, the rock structure now stands isolated like a giant pot some 3 metres or more in height with an opening at the top. It is a natural wizard's cave to delight imaginations of all ages.

The Gun Point peninsula has the greatest concentration of potholes anywhere in Ontario, and a recent geological theory has attempted to explain their existence.

A feature article in the summer 1993 *Seasons*, the quarterly magazine of the Federation of Ontario Naturalists, popularized a striking new explanation. It suggests that the potholes were created "in weeks or days—perhaps even hours" when the enormous weight of the glaciers pressing down on the meltwater beneath the ice caused the water to explode out at weak spots at the edge of the ice sheets. Explains Phil Kor, a geologist with the Ministry of Natural Resources, "When the rushing floodwater encountered the abrupt cliffs of the escarpment, great turbulence in the flow drilled out the potholes...very quickly."

Whether or not this theory will stand the scrutiny of scientists, it has opened a fascinating new interpretation for the layman. Even on an area as well researched as the Niagara Escarpment, the quest for explanations continues.

Soon the trail reaches a logging track, which it follows out to a cottage road east of the village of Lion's Head. The path swings left on the road for about 300 metres. Then, where the main trail and the road turn sharply right, the blue-blazed Ilse Hanel Trail heads directly south on a laneway. This trail was formerly the main trail and leads across the peninsula for 4 kilometres, frequently on old logging tracks. The plastic disks mark an extensive cross-country ski network; watch carefully for the hiking blazes. After about an hour's walking, you emerge from the bush and cross an open meadow to reach the yellow-blazed trail upon which you began the hike. A short distance to the right is your car.

The trail network in the middle of the peninsula gives you the opportunity to create other loops and is especially handy for the hiker who is using McKay's Harbour as a base for a weekend's adventure.

The McKay's Harbour Side Trail is a short yellow-blazed route about 1 kilometre long. From the main trail just above the campsite, it climbs the escarpment on the gradual slope of an old logging road to intersect the Inland Trail. By following this route either left or right, two small loops are created, the northern one 4.2 kilometres, and the southern one 7.2 kilometres.

A short distance off the southern loop, another yellow-blazed trail leads to a historical curiosity, a geodetic benchmark located on the 45th parallel, halfway from the equator to the North Pole! Maitland Warder remembers the construction of this marker in the 1930s. These benchmarks were used by surveyors and map makers in the days before satellites to ensure accurate calculation of distances across the land. At that time, the forest cover was low, as the land was still recovering from the ravages of intensive logging. A local man was hired to cut a cart track to the high point of land, and a thirty-metre wooden tower was erected from which to view other towers on the distant horizon. It was the time of the Great Depression and Mr. Warder remembers the pangs of envy with which the local residents viewed the workers' supplies. The government had provided the crew with an entire crate of oranges at a time when such a thing was beyond the imagination of most members of the community.

The Inland Trail gives you an alternative route across the peninsula during stormy weather, when the main route along the cliff edge to the east could be dangerous. It is also a pleasant woodland walk through a mature maple-birch forest. In springtime, the trilliums are especially attractive, and in the fall, the coloured leaves glow in the autumn sunshine.

Gun Point

Winter at Tamarac Island sawmill circa 1900. Timber from the sawmill building forms part of the present-day dining room at Tamarac Island Inn, Stokes Bay. The inn is accessible by road and well worth a visit.
– Credit: Bev Matheson

The Gun Point peninsula also has a network of excellent cross-country ski trails. Maps are available at local outlets in Lion's Head, and parking is provided at the high school. The trails are colour-coded and, except for near the escarpment, not difficult. But beware of the danger of the cliff edge in winter; it is a long fall to the rocks below.

In its few years of existence, the Gun Point Loop has become one of the most popular hikes on the Bruce. Shirley Teasdale, author of *Hiking Ontario's Heartland*, refers to the northern part of this route as "an absolutely spectacular hike offering stunning views that cannot be surpassed anywhere in the world." It is a great introduction to the rich variety of the peninsula landscape. Of course, the ruggedness of the terrain makes the loop a complete day's outing for many hikers, but the McKay Harbour campsite is a temptation to extend your trip. When combined with the possibilities of the Inland Trail, there are enough alternatives to provide excitement for any hiker.

"The Bruce Beckons"
The Trails of Cyprus Lake
and Dorcas Bay

The spectacular scenery of the Bruce Peninsula made a deep impression on W. Sherwood Fox, author of *The Bruce Beckons*. "The Lord God who planted a garden eastward in Eden did not forget to plant a garden northward as well. It is none other than the great clear-cut promontory of the Great Lakes."

Many hikers have discovered that rugged beauty, which, enthralled Fox. So suspect, though, that many others, intimidated by the challenge of the upper Bruce, tend to stick to the southern areas of the province. If this is the case, it is a needless precaution, for the trails of Cyprus Lake are accessible to all and offer a splendid opportunity to explore one of the most spectacular parts of the entire Bruce Trail. They will take you along the edge of sheer cliffs, down tiered limestone ledges and across white boulder beaches to the clear waters of Georgian Bay. If you are fit, you will be able to climb down into a vast sea cave, and if you have strong nerves, you can stand on a slab of overhanging rock 30 metres above the water looking out over majestic headland and rocky promontory to the rugged fortresses of the offshore islands.

On the Lake Huron side of the peninsula, where the land slides gently into the lake, there are wonderful sights of a different kind. Dorcas Bay, one of the larger bays, is part of the Bruce Peninsula National Park. It is very shallow, and along its edge, the rocks display glacial striae, long scratches gouged into the limestone by the harder rocks frozen in the glacial ice as it moved across from the northeast. Singing Sands Beach is a perfect place to swim. Along its sandy shore, the depth of the water increases slowly as you walk out, and the bay is so shallow that the summer sun can heat it like a bathtub. However, if you are a lover of wildlife, the main attraction of Dorcas Bay is the nature reserve, with its variety of inhabitants, especially the orchid species—more than fifteen of them.

Cyprus Lake & Dorcas Bay

17

Trail Length: **5 kilometres**

Time: **3 hours (with time for exploration)**

Grade: **Moderate-strenuous**

Access: **Follow Highway 6 to the Bruce Peninsula National Park (Cyprus Lake entrance), about 10 kilometres south of Tobermory. Drive via the park road to the Head of the Trails.**

Map: ***Guide to the Bruce Trail:* map 40: Tobermory**

Parking: **At the Head of the Trails. (A day-use fee may be charged in the National Park.)**

Begin from the Head of the Trails, where parking and a map are available. The Georgian Bay Trail is a good place to start. It has been widened and the treadway groomed to allow easy access to the spectacular scenery of the shoreline.

Just after the intersection with the Marr Lake Trail (on which you will be returning), stop at the interpretive display that explains the Horse

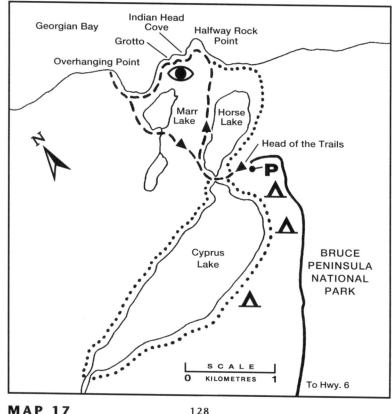

Cyprus Lake & Dorcas Bay

Lake sinks. The surface stream that drained Horse Lake was captured by joints in the dolostone, and the water now flows through underground passages to emerge ninety minutes later as springs on the shore of Marr Lake. In the spring, five drain holes create a whirlpool action somewhat like a bathtub draining. In the low water of summer, these sinks frequently dry up.

The trail passes through a variety of forest cover and, just before the shoreline, climbs over several limestone ridges. These bioherms, as they are called, are the remains of ancient coral reefs from the warm inland sea of 450 million years ago.

At the shoreline, interpretive panels explain "the battle zone," where the wave energy of the bay conflicts with the nearly vertical dolostone rock. The result is the bowling-ball-sized cobbles that can make for difficult hiking along the beaches. From the shoreline, the escarpment continues to drop underwater for a further 170 metres to the deepest point in Georgian Bay. The cliffs visible along the shore to the right are Cave Point and, in the distance, Cabot Head. To the left is Halfway Rock Point and the route we shall be following. Anything between the water's edge and the thick cedar forest can be explored. The widest path is the white-blazed Bruce Trail, 30 metres back from the water, but the more difficult but scenically rewarding paths follow the shoreline.

Beyond the point lies Indian Head Cove, a tiny but beautiful bay with a white cobble beach, one of the favourite places in the park for swimming and snorkelling in the clean, clear water. Be sure to look back at the point, where nature has etched an overturned canoe and the proud profile of an Indian face. In the cove, 400 million-year-old fossils, once born in a coral sea, now lie exposed. Orange and pink-brown lichens, primitive living plants, are widespread on the rock face. Tiny ferns, cedars and blue harebells grow in pockets of soil.

To the west of the cove are the grottoes, water-formed caves that are embedded in the limestone body of the escarpment. Through time, their interiors have been enlarged by wave action to such an extent that the ceilings weakened and eventually collapsed. Natural Arch, the first grotto you come to, was formed by this process.

As you travel westward along the trail, you reach a true grotto. You will be astonished by its size. Climb down and explore its interior; it is about 20 metres long and 9 metres wide. You will be deceived by the appearance of the water's depth; near the back of the cave it is between 9 and 12 metres deep. An underwater entrance, visible as a light patch, leads to the bay; frequently, you see divers exploring this connection to the open water. In the warmth of summer, the grotto can provide a unique swimming hole. (The climb up again is fairly strenuous, so be prudent.)

Back on the trail, you soon come to a large boulder beach, 120 metres wide and 150 metres long. First, you cross a jumble of limestone slabs and rocks of all sizes. Water trickling through the stones comes from Marr Lake. Be sure to note the carpet of poison ivy clinging to the bare rocks— beautiful, but beware!

After you cross the stream you ascend three or four terraces. These were formed by a postglacial ancestor of Georgian Bay as it receded to its present level. In pockets in the rock, you will find clumps of small magenta flowers with dissected leaves. These are a wild geranium.

Before heading back via the Marr Lake Trail, continue on a short distance to Overhanging Point, according to the editors of the *Guide to the Bruce Trail*, "one of the most spectacular points of the Bruce Trail." Here the dolostone cap-rock has been left unsupported as the underlying limestone has eroded away. Eventually, the point will succumb to the forces of time and gravity and tumble to the base of the cliff face. It is a strange but exhilarating feeling to stand suspended on a metre of rock projecting into the air 30 metres above the water! A short distance back from the edge is a tunnel through which you can descend to the underlying shelf. The climb up again through the hole is not difficult. Known as Lord Hunt's Tunnel, it gives you an opportunity figuratively to descend through time.

Afterwards, go back to the last boulder beach and return to the parking lot via the Marr Lake Trail. It first climbs the ancient coral reefs and then levels out in the cool dampness of the forest. A variety of flowering plants provides a continuous parade of blooms throughout the summer. Information concerning the flora and fauna is available at the national park entrance or from the interpretive staff.

Other options from the Head of the Trails are the Cyprus Lake Trail and the Horse Lake Trail. The 7-kilometre Cypress Lake Trail passes over less demanding terrain as it circles the inland lake. Several orchids are found along its path, including lady's-slipper, coral root, purple-fringed orchis and ladies' tresses. Watch for the remains of several large old tree stumps, the evidence of past logging and forest fires from the early 1900s. The Horse Lake Trail, 1 kilometre in length, moves from the lake's marshy shoreline through a cedar forest to a cobble beach on Georgian Bay. Watch for great blue herons, caspian terns and waterfowl along the lake. The shaded section of the cedar forest is home to a small orchid known as rattlesnake plantain. Look for its two-tone leaves hugging the ground.

Although summer is undoubtedly the time to first become introduced to this area, the other seasons have their unique charms. In November, it is not uncommon to see a northeaster bring waves splashing right over the top of the high cliffs of the escarpment. The waves created by a wind of more than thirty knots are spectacular.

In the winter especially, when the Bruce is at its wildest and most rugged, the Cyprus Lake area is a lonely and beautiful place. Floating ice cakes, each weighing tons, hammer the cliffs. A thick coating of ice, the legacy of the waves, covers the rocks. There is an obvious element of danger, and anyone skiing or hiking the trail should have suitable touring equipment. But the view of Georgian Bay from the cliffs in winter makes it worth the struggle.

Trail Length: **2 kilometres**

Time: **2 hours**

Grade: **Easy**

Access: **From Highway 6, about 10 kilometres south of Tobermory, immediately north of the Cyprus Lake entrance to the Bruce Peninsula National Park, turn west on the Dorcas Bay Road. Drive about 1 kilometre and turn right (north) at the park sign indicating the Singing Sands Beach.**

Map: ***Guide to the Bruce Trail:* map 40: Tobermory**

Parking: **Park near the north end of the parking area and walk across the footbridge.**

On July 18, 1992, at the entrance to the Dorcas Bay Nature Reserve, a cairn was unveiled by the Sierra Club and the Canadian Parks Service to commemorate the visits to the area by John Muir in the 1860s. Muir was the father of parks in North America and one of the first naturalists to recognize the richness of the Bruce. The parks and reserves established there owe much to his rich legacy.

Other naturalists also deserve credit for the preservation of the Bruce, among them Malcolm (Mac) Kirk who, in 1962, persuaded the bankrupt owner of property on Dorcas Bay to give him a three-month option on the land for one dollar. He then turned to the Federation of Ontario Naturalists (FON) for help in raising the twenty thousand dollars needed to purchase the property. Eventually, all the money was raised, and the nature reserve established.

From the parking area, walk across a small footbridge that spans a reversing stream; water flows to and then from Lake Huron as the lake's level oscillates. It may take up to an hour to see this change in water level, known as a *seiche.*

Once across the bridge, you enter the Dorcas Bay Nature Reserve. There is no office and no guide. A sign simply announces: Walkers welcome. Please leave plants untouched for others to see.

Unlike other hikes in this book, this one has no specifically defined route. An old dirt road branches in two directions; the left fork parallels the shore and the right leads to Highway 6. Both invite exploration, as does the Backland Trail, which meanders in a leisurely way between the two.

You will find enormous ecological variety at Dorcas Bay, from sand beaches and dunes to limestone outcrops, wet meadows, fens and woodlands. In this diversity of habitats is a corresponding variety of plants, some extremely rare.

The most significant habitat is the fen, an alkaline, nutrient-rich wetland dominated by sedges and rushes. It nourishes orchids such as rose pogonia and showy lady's-slipper. At Dorcas Bay, orchids are said to grow in greater abundance and with more diversity than anywhere else on the

Cyprus Lake & Dorcas Bay

A ferry heads out of Tobermory harbour around the turn of the century.
– Credit: Sheila Gatis

continent. Also found in the fen are curiosities such as the insect-eating pitcher plant, sundew and bladderwort.

The open sand dunes receive the greatest number of visitors. Underneath the jack pines is some of the most interesting flora of the reserve. In May, dwarf lake irises cover the ground, and in the first half of June, the beautiful yellow lady's-slipper grows in almost weedlike abundance along the paths.

This web of vegetation creates a habitat for wildlife. Warblers nest in the woodlands and turkey vultures soar overhead. In the dunes, the eastern massasauga rattlesnake usually keeps shyly to itself; it is unlikely that you will see one. In the springtime, wildlife also includes blackflies and mosquitoes; for protection, hats, long sleeves and insect repellent are essential.

Why not experience the beauty of the Bruce for yourself? You may fall under the spell that Sherwood Fox describes: "At his first sight of the Bruce Peninsula the visitor cannot but be aware of a land astonishingly unlike any he has ever seen before." And no matter whether you are enthralled by the savage beauty of the escarpment cliffs or by the rare and diverse inhabitants of the nature reserve, one thing is easy to predict: Once you have seen the Bruce, you will want to return again and again.

"Full Fathom Five Thy History Lies"
The Trails of Flowerpot Island

Trail Length: **3 kilometres**

Time: **3 hours (with time for exploration)**

Grade: **Easy-moderate**

Access: **By tour boat from Tobermory's Little Tub Harbour. (Some tour boats first take you to the Big Tub shipwrecks.)**

Map: **A trail map is available at the National Park Visitor Centre in Tobermory and on the island.**

Parking: **In Tobermory at the Community Centre. From here, it is a short walk to the harbour.**

The harbour village of Tobermory sits at the tip of the Bruce Peninsula. Named after a community on the Isle of Mull in Scotland, it still has a fishermen's cove setting. At its heart are two deep natural harbours, known affectionately as Little Tub and Big Tub.

A century ago, the harbours were bustling with the commerce of sawmills and the fishing fleet. Today, they host turtleback fishing tugs and, in summer, hundreds of sleek sailboats and luxury yachts. Lining Little Tub harbour, you will find docks, shops, restaurants, lodges, the National Parks Visitor Centre and the loading facilities for the Chi-Cheemaun, the huge car ferry to Manitoulin Island. One side of the harbour has a raised walkway, a good spot to stand and watch the sun set over the Tobermory Islands.

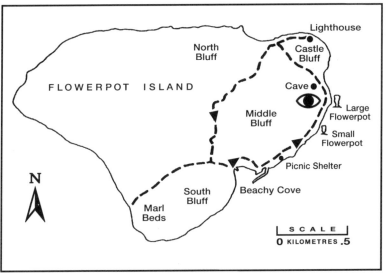

MAP 18

18

Flowerpot Island

Sightseers gather under the sea stack on Flowerpot Island.
– Credit: County of Grey–Owen Sound Museum

The Niagara Escarpment disappears underwater off Tobermory and reappears on Manitoulin Island. In between, it surfaces only at intervals as groups of rocky islands. Nineteen of these make up Fathom Five, Canada's first national marine park. In the clear, deep but treacherous water that surrounds them lie over twenty historic shipwrecks. On almost any morning in Little Tub harbour, you will see divers suiting up for a day of exploration.

The only island that is readily accessible is Flowerpot Island, 6 kilometres from Tobermory. It is a rare, enchanted place with a thousand charms

Flowerpot Island

18

awaiting your discovery. Arrange for a tour boat to take you over and pick you up a few hours or, if you like, a few days later. You can stay at one of the six primitive campsites nestled beside the waters of Beachey Cove, but remember, they are available only on a first-come, first-served basis. If you do manage to stay, you'll find that after the last of the tour boats has left for the day, the evening tranquillity is a memorable experience.

The four bluffs that dominate Flowerpot Island are fossilized coral reefs. This rock, stronger than limestone, resisted the scraping of the glacier that removed the surrounding rock. Immediately after the retreat of the ice, each of the bluffs was a separate island, rising above the water. The rest of the island has slowly emerged as water levels have fallen.

Of course, the flowerpots that give the island its name are the main attraction. These are sea stacks, pillars of rock eroded by wave action and weathering. But so distinctive is their shape that throughout human history their presence has given the island a mystical charm. In *Tall Tales and Collections of the Georgian Bay*, Melba Croft relates the myth of their origin:

> Many moons ago, when the Indian people owned all the land from the Manitoulin to the Blue Mountains, tribes lived within a few arrows' flight of one another. There were many wars. Sometimes young braves of one tribe fell in love with maidens of another. This was not good, for each tribe was very proud and independent. Toward the end of the eighteenth century the son of a powerful tribal chief fell in love with the daughter of another chief, and ran away with her.
>
> The lovers travelled by canoe. Soon the maiden's father assembled his warriors and set off after them. Now as he paddled swiftly the young lover remembered the Island of the Caves and hurried there to hide his sweetheart in a deep cave. But the maiden's father also thought of this and soon caught up with the pair. The young brave was killed and the maiden died of a broken heart.
>
> Since that time, Indians have called the island the Island of the Flower Pots, and they claim that the two flower-pot formations are the stone spirits of the young Indian lovers. To them the island is a forbidden place, and they will not set foot on its shore.

Today, the flowerpots can be reached by a short well-marked trail from the dock. They stand massive and improbable, in bold relief beside the clear blue waters. One is a tall, graceful sculpture, 12 metres high, while the smaller, at 7 metres, is a fat flowerpot with a cedar tree and small shrubs clinging to its side. With a little imagination, you can see them as real flowerpots, although the only flowers they support are hardy blue harebells.

The cliffs out of which the flowerpots evolved now stand back from the shore. Centuries of erosion have worked on them. The hard dolostone cap-rock resisted the elements, but the surrounding rock did not. As lake levels dropped, erosion ate away lower and lower into the softer limestone, until eventually the pillars were severed from the bluff. Then, in the 1930s, the Parks Service reinforced the stems and capped the tops with concrete to slow erosion.

From the lookout just beyond the huge boulder in the path, you can see future flowerpots in the making. In the cliff extending into the water are joints, vertical splits in the rock, formed as the limestone dried and shrank. Waves surge into these crevices and wear away the rock on both sides. The space will get wider and wider until a section of the cliff is separated from the shore. It will take many generations, but these cliff fragments may eventually stand out as small flowerpots.

A series of caves on the east and northeast sides of the islands offers further evidence that water levels were once much higher. These caves are now at heights ranging from 8 to 30 metres above the talus slopes and ancient beaches. Today, similar caves are being formed along the South Bluff; some day these will be reminders of the present level of Georgian Bay.

You can reach one of the caves via a short trail and stairs just past the large flowerpot. From a viewing platform in the cave, you can marvel at the power of time and water. The roof and walls are part of the ancient coral reef, and the rock debris on the floor is evidence of continuing erosion. The serious spelunker is permitted to explore the caves, but only after registering at the main dock. Minimum requirements to enter a cave include sturdy footwear, a light for every member of the party and hard hats.

Continue on the well-marked loop trail and be sure to visit the lighthouse on Castle Bluff on the northeast corner of the island. If you happen to be there when the mist is thick, it is a haunting experience to listen to the booming foghorn echoed back by passing ships. If it is a fine evening you can watch the sun set over Fitzwilliam Island, 21 kilometres to the northwest. Directly east across the shipping channel is Bear's Rump Island, a microcosm of the Bruce Peninsula with its steep cliffs at one end and sloping shoreline at the other. Between is the deepest point in the marine park, at 90 metres.

In front of the terrace beach sit the two lighthouse keepers' homes. Today, they are empty, victims of a modern technology which has automated all these stations on the Great Lakes. They now represent a bygone era when two families lived here together, isolated from the mainland. They used a cave to refrigerate their supplies and a clearing in the woods to farm for fresh produce. You will pass by that field on the inland trail; today, it is quickly reverting to forest as the poplars reclaim the land.

From the lighthouse, continue on the loop trail to the interior of the island. As it slowly winds up Middle Bluff, the trail enters a sheltered community where unusual plants thrive. In this gallery of ferns and mosses, "leftovers" from the ice age are found. Along the north side, the climate is especially cool and moist. Among the numerous species of ferns you will find maidenhair ferns, growing in rich shaded soils, and spleenworts growing in the moist areas.

If you can, visit the island in early June when the orchids are in bloom. Some twenty-eight types can be found, many of which are tiny and inconspicuous. The fairest and rarest of them all is the exquisite Calypso. Seldom rising above shoelace level, the solitary pink, white, golden-

At the entrance to the Great Caves on Flowerpot Island.
– Credit: County of Grey–Owen Sound Museum

yellow and reddish-brown flower has its lower petal striped like a dainty fairy slipper, surrounded by several mauve-pink petals and sepals. The famous American conservationist, John Muir, spent two years in the 1860s studying the botany of the Niagara Escarpment. He later recounted that one of the two most significant moments of his entire life was his discovery of a Calypso orchid in Ontario; its beauty was such that he wept for joy.

If the flowers seem to form a Garden of Eden, then this Eden also has its snakes. Because of its isolation, few skunks, weasels or raccoons have migrated across the water. Without predators and with abundant nesting sites and food, a healthy population of garter, water and milk snakes has developed. But there is no need for trepidation; the massasauga rattlesnake, although found on the mainland, never made it to the island.

Before you return to Beachey Cove and the dock, walk southwest on the Marl Bed Trail. The marl bed is a shallow soft-bottomed pond, but the adjacent cobblestone beach indicates that it was once a small bay. Today, water drains off the surrounding slopes and collects in the hollow. It is rich in dissolved limestone, which settles out as mucky, claylike marl. Although the water is too alkaline for plant growth, the neighbouring area is home to very specialized plants and animals. Numerous wildflowers grow along its fringe.

Finally, when you get back to the main deck to wait for your tour boat, enjoy the sun on the limestone shelf that runs along the south shore to the flowerpots. This is the best place on the island for picnicking and swimming, though the waters of northern Georgian Bay are always cold. And remember to keep an eye on your watch to ensure that you do not miss your boat. It's a long swim to town!

Flowerpot Island

ACCOMMODATION AND DINING
~ AUTHORS' CHOICE ~

(Listed in order from south to north)

DUNDAS
Bed and Breakfast
MARGARET AND JOHN CAREY
Glenwood
42 Osler Drive
Dundas, Ontario L9H 4B1
Tel: (905) 627-0596

CAMPBELLVILLE
Bed and Breakfast
JACK AND NANCY RAITHBY
Winklewood Lane
RR#2,
Campbellville, Ontario L0P 1B0
Tel: (905) 854-0527

CATARACT
Bed and Breakfast
RODNEY AND JENNIFER HOUGH
Cataract Inn
Lunch: noon–2:30 p.m. (Fri.–Sun.)
Dinner: 5:30–9:00 p.m.
Closed Mon. and Tues.
RR#2 Alton, Ontario, L0N 1A0
Licensed, LLBO
Tel: (519) 927-3033

HOCKLEY
Bed and Breakfast
JANET DOBROWSKI,
HEATHER SHEEHAN
and GAY HALPENNY
The Driveshed
Hockley Village
Lunch, Tea
Take-out food
General Store
RR#5
Orangeville, Ontario L9W 2Z2
Tel: (519) 942-3130

HOCKLEY
Bed and do-it-yourself breakfast
DAVID MEYNELL
Hockley's Country Inn
Lunch: 10 a.m.–3 p.m.
Dinner 5:30 p.m. until closing
RR#5
Orangeville, Ontario L9W 2Z2
Licensed, LLBO
Tel: (519) 941-8857

MONO CENTRE
CAROL AND MIKE HALL
Mono Cliffs Inn
Restaurant: Lunch and Dinner
Peter's Cellar Pub: Light meals
Open Thurs.–Sun.
RR#1
Mono Centre, Ontario L9W 2Y8
Licensed, LLBO
Tel: (519) 941-5109

CRAIGLEITH
Chez Michel Restaurant
Lunch and Dinner
Closed Tues.
Pinery Plaza
Craigleith, Ontario
Licensed, LLBO
Tel: (705) 445-9441

KIMBERLEY
Bed and Breakfast
GRAHAM AND MARY LAMONT
Lamont Guest Home
Meals by request
Box 24
Kimberley, Ontario N0C 1G0
Tel: (519) 599-5605

KIMBERLEY
Bed and Breakfast
BEV AND RON WREN
Wren's Mountain Farm
Meals by request
RR#1
Kimberley, Ontario N0C 1G0
Tel: (519) 599-5098

Accommodation and Dining ~ Authors's Choice

CLARKSBURG
Bed and Breakfast
KAREN AND NORM STEWART
Hillside
Meals by request
Box 72
Clarksburg, Ontario N0H 1J0
Tel: (519) 599-5523

THORNBURY
Bed and Breakfast
SALLY PEARSON
The Mill Pond
Box 254
Thornbury, Ontario N0H 2P0
Tel: (519) 599-6717

THORNBURY
The Mill Cafe
Lunch and Dinner
Open 7 days a week
12 Bridge Street
Thornbury, Ontario N0H 2P0
Licensed, LLBO
Tel: (519) 599-2550

CHATSWORTH
Bed and Breakfast
BETTE AND BARRY LEWIN
Hollyhock Acres
RR#2
Chatsworth, Ontario N0H 1G0
Tel: (519) 794-3547

STOKES BAY
Bed and Breakfast
BEV AND MEL MATHESON
Tamarac Island Inn
Lunch and Dinner
Stokes Bay, Ontario N0H 2M0
Licensed, LLBO
Tel: (519) 592-5810

Bruce Peninsula National Park
Box 189, Tobermory, Ontario N0H 2R0
Tel: (519) 596-2233

Bruce Peninsula Tourism Association
P.O. Box 269, Wiarton, Ontario N0H 2T0
Tel: 1-800-268-3838
(519) 596-2452

Bruce Trail Association
P.O. Box 857
Hamilton, Ontario L8N 3N9
Tel: (905) 529-6821 (24-hr answering machine)
1-800-665-HIKE
Fax: (905) 529-6823

Chippewas of Nawash Band Office
R.R. #5, Wiarton, Ontario N0H 2T0
Tel: (519) 534-1689
(519) 534-0571 (park office)

Credit Valley Conservation Authority
1255 Derry Road West
Meadowvale, Ontario L5N 6R4
Tel: 1-800-668-5557
(905) 670-1615

Fathom Five National Marine Park
Box 189, Tobermory, Ontario N0H 2R0
Tel: (519) 596-2510

Federation of Ontario Naturalists
335 Lesmill Road
Don Mills, Ontario M3B 2W8
Tel: (416) 444-8419

Georgian Triangle Tourist Association and Convention Bureau
601 First Street,
Collingwood, Ontario L9Y 4L2
Tel: 1-800-461-1300
(705) 445-7722 (tourist information)
(705) 445-0748 (accom./reservation)
Fax: (705) 444-6158

Grey-Bruce Tourist Association
R.R. #5, Owen Sound, Ontario N4K 5N7
Tel: (519) 371-2071
1-800-265-3127
Fax: (519) 371-5315

Grey-Sauble Conservation Authority
R.R. #4, Owen Sound, Ontario N4K 5N6
Tel: (519) 376-3076

(continued on next page)

**Greater Hamilton Tourist and
Convention Services**
Economic Development Department
127 King Street East,
Hamilton, Ontario L8N 1B1
Tel: (905) 546-4222

Halton Region Conservation Authority
P.O. Box 1097, Station B,
Burlington, Ontario L7P 3S9
Tel: (905) 336-1158

Hamilton Region Conservation Authority
Box 7099
838 Mineral Springs Road
Ancaster, Ontario L9G 3L3
Tel: (905) 525-2181

Hike Ontario!
1220 Sheppard Avenue East
Willowdale, Ontario, M2K 2X1
Tel: (416) 495-3417
Fax: (416) 495-4310

Huronia Tourist Association
Simcoe County Building
Midhurst, Ontario L0L 1X0
Tel: (705) 726-9300
1-800-461-4343

Kolapore Ski Trails
Box 6647, Station A
Toronto, Ontario M5W 1X4

Meaford Chamber of Commerce
Box 1298, Meaford, Ontario N0H 1Y0
Tel: (519) 538-1640

Niagara Escarpment Commission
232 Guelph Street
Georgetown, Ontario L7G 4B1
Tel: (905) 877-5191

Niagara Falls Parks Commission
Box 150, Niagara Falls, Ontario L2E 6T2
Tel: (905) 356-2241

**Niagara Falls Canada Visitor
and Convention Bureau**
5433 Victoria Avenue
Niagara Falls, Ontario L2G 3L1
Tel: (905) 356-6061

**Niagara Peninsula Conservation
Authority**
Centre Street
Allanburg, Ontario L0S 1A0
Tel: (905) 227-1013

**Nottawasaga Valley Conservation
Authority**
R.R.#1, Angus, Ontario L0M 1B0
Tel: (705) 424-1479

**Ontario Ministry of Natural Resources
Public Information Centre**
Queen's Park
Toronto, Ontario M7A 1W3
Tel: (416) 314-2000
Fax: (416) 314-1593

Ontario Travel
Queen's Park
Toronto, Ontario M7A 2E5
Tel: (416) 314-0944
1-800-ONTARIO
Fax: (416) 314-7372

**Ontario Ministry of Transport and
Communications**
1201 Wilson Avenue
Downsview, Ontario M3M 1J8
Tel: (416) 235-4339

Ontario Northland Marine Services
Tel: (519) 596-2510 (Tobermory
Terminal)
(705) 859-3161 (South Baymouth
Terminal)
1-800-265-3163

Orangeville Chamber of Commerce
Box 101, Orangeville, Ontario L9W 2Z5
Tel: (519) 941-0490

**Owen Sound Visitor and
Convention Bureau**
832 2nd Avenue East
Owen Sound, Ontario N4K 2H3
Tel: (519) 371-9833

Royal Botanical Gardens
Box 399, Hamilton, Ontario L8N 3H8
Tel: (905) 527-1158
1-800-263-8450

Tobermory Chamber of Commerce
Box 250, Tobermory, Ontario N0H 2R0
Tel: (519) 596-2452

Wiarton Clerk's Office
Box 310,
Wiarton, Ontario N0H 2T0
Tel: (519) 534-1400 (winter)
(519) 534-2592 (summer)

Useful Addresses

BIBLIOGRAPHY

Armitage, Andrew. *Owen Sound: The Day The Governor-General Came To Town and Other Tales.* Erin, Ontario: The Boston Mills Press, 1979.

Beaumont, Ralph. *Alton, A Pictorial History.* Erin, Ontario: The Boston Mills Press, 1974.

————. *Cataract and the Forks of the Credit, A Pictorial History.* Erin, Ontario: Boston Mills Press, 1974.

Brooksbank, Jack. *The Hockley Story.* Hockley Village: Jacques Bea Studios, 1988.

Bruce Trail Association. *Bruce Trail News.*

————. *Guide to the Bruce Trail.* 18th ed., 1992.

Campbell, Marjorie Freeman. *A Mountain and a City: The Story of Hamilton.* Toronto, Ontario: McClelland and Stewart Limited, 1966.

Chapman, L.T., and Putnam, D.F. *The Physiography of Southern Ontario.* Ministry of Natural Resources, 1984.

Croft, Melba Morris. *Tall Tales and Legends of Georgian Bay.* Owen Sound, Ontario: 1961.

Davidson, T. Arthur. *A New History of Grey County.* The Grey County Historical Society, 1972.

Federation of Ontario Naturalists. *Seasons.*

Fox, William Sherwood. *The Bruce Beckons.* Toronto, Ontario: University of Toronto Press, 1952.

Gillard, William, and Tooke, Thomas. *The Niagara Escarpment: From Tobermory to Niagara Falls.* Toronto, Ontario: University of Toronto Press, 1975.

Grimwood, Paul. *The Hermitage.* Hamilton Region Conservation Authority, 1976.

Hilts, S., Kirk, M., Reid, R., et al. *Islands of Green: Natural Heritage Protection in Ontario.* Toronto, Ontario: Ontario Heritage Foundation, 1986.

Keough, Pat and Rosemary. *The Niagara Escarpment—A Portfolio.* Toronto, Ontario: Stoddart, 1990.

Kosydar, Richard and Eleanore. *Natural Landscapes of the Dundas Valley.* Ancaster, Ontario: Tierceron Design, 1989.

Leitch, Adelaide. *Into the High Country.* Orangeville, Ontario: Corporation of the County of Dufferin, 1975.

Niagara Escarpment Commission. *Cuesta.*

Smith, Paul G.R., Kirk, Donald, Cundiff, Brad. *A Field Guide to the Nature Reserves of the Federation of Ontario Naturalists.* Don Mills, Ontario: 1991.

Stephens, Lorina and Gary. *Touring the Giant's Rib: A Guide to the Niagara Escarpment.* Toronto, Ontario: Stoddart, 1993.

Teasdale, Shirley. *Hiking Ontario's Heartland.* Vancouver, British Columbia: Whitecap, 1993.

Tovell, Walter M. *Guide to the Geology of the Niagara Escarpment.* Niagara Escarpment Commission, 1992.

————. *The Niagara Escarpment.* Toronto, Ontario: University of Toronto Press, 1965.

University of Toronto Outing Club. *Kolapore Uplands Wilderness Ski Trails.* 13th ed., 1992.

Warder, Walter. *Between You and Me and The Gatepost. A Historic View of The Lion's Head Area.* Lion's Head, Ontario: 1977.

Woodhouse, Roy T. *A Short History of Dundas.* Town of Dundas, 1947.

INDEX OF PLACE NAMES